MARVELS OF ENGINEERING

MARVELS

OF ENGINEERING

NATIONAL GEOGRAPHIC
WASHINGTON, D.C.

Contents

Preceding pages: An ancient engineering marvel in both size and scale, the Roman Colosseum owes its longevity to the strength of Roman concrete.

Right: New York's 1903 Flatiron Building, supported entirely by a steel frame, typifies the first skyscrapers. Its stone facade is simply decorative.

W. 26 ST.

1: OVERCOMING

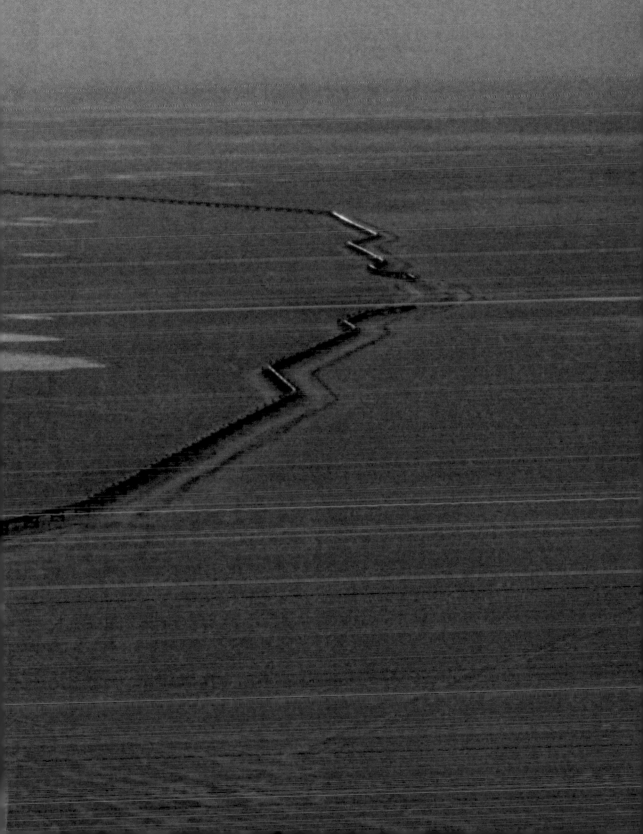

DISTANCE

Roads
Waterways
Bridges
Railroads
Pipelines

THEY ARE AT ONCE THE LIFELINES of modern civilization and the means for its dispersal: roads and highways that carry trucks and automobiles; canals and inland waterways that ship commodities; bridges that leap rivers and canyons; railroads that move freight; and pipelines that transport water, natural gas, and petroleum. For civil engineers, the unimpeded movement of goods and people is among the most fundamental objectives, one that embraces a host of challenges.

Building large structures invariably requires excavation, and moving earth, even with today's arsenal of equipment, is not easy. Hills must be resculptured to accommodate a highway, a river diverted while a dam is constructed. But rearranging the topography is only one step in the construction process. It begins with an investigation of the proposed site, during which routes are surveyed and mapped. Engineers do test drillings and use the resulting core samples to determine whether the soil along a proposed pipeline is stable or whether the underlying bedrock can support the foundation of a bridge. Still later in the process, building materials are chosen after climate, site selection, function, appearance, economics, and other factors are analyzed.

A range of other criteria must be factored in to the equation, depending on the type of structure. In designing a road or a bridge, engineers must consider every contingency: the volume of traffic, the kinds of vehicles, how fast they travel, the effects of wind and weather, and the impact of tides and currents on underwater foundations.

In waterway design, channels must have either moderate gradients or locks to move vessels from one water level to another; bank erosion is a concern. Railroads must be designed with limited gradients. The track and roadbed must withstand the weight of passing trains, as well as the dynamic loads imposed by the impact and sway of speeding locomotives.

Major works of civil engineering are hallmarks of civilization. Often, like the Roman aqueducts and first transcontinental railroad, they play vital roles in a nation's or a region's development and can radically alter the landscape. Well designed and built, they serve as symbols of their eras and evidence of human mastery over seemingly insurmountable challenges. ■

Preceding pages: The Trans-Alaska Pipeline zigzags across snow-covered tundra.

Left: Lethbridge Viaduct in Alberta, Canada a mile long and 314 feet high—replaced an earlier rail line that crossed the valley on 20 wooden bridges.

Roads

ALTHOUGH THE ROMANS WERE THE BEST road builders of the ancient world, they were not the first. The Persians and Chinese had roads as early as 500 B.C., although most of theirs were primitive by Roman standards.

The Romans were no-nonsense road builders and masters of cut-and-fill engineering: Working without benefit of dynamite and bulldozers, they sliced through hills, cracking rocks first by heating them with fire and then by dousing them with cold water, and spanned ravines with arched bridges. With the collapse of the Roman Empire, Rome's magnificent highway system fell into ruin.

Modern road building began in 18th-century Britain and France with the development of new hard-surface roads having proper drainage. The coming of motor vehicles in the 20th century made earlier roadways obsolete. New and better road surfaces using concrete or asphalt proved best for vehicles with rubber tires, and superhighways covering long distances made travel easier and faster. ■

BEGUN IN 1811 and completed some 40 years later, the U.S. National Road stretched more than 600 miles between Cumberland, Maryland, and Vandalia, Illinois, and helped encourage western settlement. It got its start as an old Indian trail and was later widened for wagons. Near Washington, Pennsylvania, in 1910, its original surface shows the wear and tear of automobile traffic but forms a solid base for future asphalt paving. This was the first U.S. highway constructed entirely with federal funds. Congress wanted not only the straightest route but also one that never exceeded a grade of five degrees. A compromise was reached: gentle curves abound.

ROMAN ROADS: The ancient Romans built roads to last, and sections of some, like the Appian Way, have endured for more than 2,000 years. The Romans recognized the need for effective drainage and elevated their roads above the surrounding terrain—creating, literally, a high way.

Major Roman highways were up to 30 feet wide and carried two traffic lanes. A surveyor laid them out and checked the road's level and course. Soldiers, slaves, and convicts provided labor, clearing brush, digging drainage ditches, and leveling the roadbed. Heavy rollers hauled by hand compacted the subsoil. Layers of stones were set into concrete and tamped down with weights. Finally, stone slabs were fitted into place and cambered (arched slightly in the center) to shed rainwater.

Over such roads freight hauled in carts or wagons moved 15 to 75 miles a day, and couriers on horseback, working in relay teams, could race nearly 150 miles in 24 hours, pausing periodically at way stations for food and fresh horses.

Roman road building began almost full-blown in 312 B.C., when the senate approved construction of the Appian Way, which ultimately became part of an extensive road system linking Rome with its outposts in Europe, the Middle East, and Africa. ■

Opposite: **A Roman road near Aleppo, Syria, still carries traffic after two millennia.**

Below: **A 50,000-mile network of roads connected outposts of the far-flung Roman Empire.**

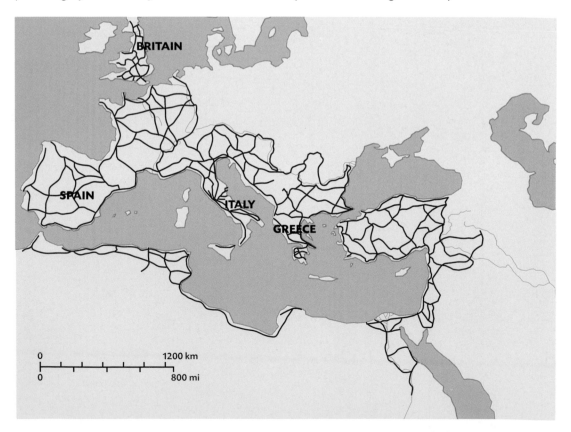

BEGINNINGS OF THE MODERN ROAD: The modern road traces its beginnings to Pierre Trésaguet, a French engineer who in 1775 developed a much lighter road than the massive, solid Roman ones. His roads were 18 feet wide and only 10 inches thick. To build them, he laid fieldstones edgewise and covered them with crushed and graded rock. Thus the subsoil, rather than thick stone slabs, which were favored by the Romans, bore the weight of traffic. Such a road was more economical to build, and it required less moving of earth.

Trésaguet's English counterpart was John Metcalf. He, too, believed in lighter roads supported by properly drained subsoil. Through one marshy section, he "floated" his road on a thick subbase of gorse and heather laid crisscross to form a firm foundation.

Two other English pioneers, Thomas Telford and John McAdam, in the 1820s and '30s perfected the use of stone sorted by size into layers and compacted into a watertight surface by passing wagons.

To achieve adequate drainage, Telford cut ditches and elevated his roads three or four feet above ground level. Large foundation stones, flat surfaces down, were placed by hand and covered by smaller stones, which carriage traffic compacted. McAdam built his roads up with several layers of rough stones, each layer decreasing in size toward the surface. Passing traffic pulverized and compacted the stones into a water-resistant surface.

Telford's and McAdam's works became standards of excellence until the coming of the automobile and the inflatable rubber tire around 1895. ■

"It is more difficult to go to Sichuan than to get into heaven," remarked an eighth-century Chinese poet. The winding road (*left*), built during the 1960s, extends more than 1,400 miles across the provinces of Sichuan and Tibet—a two-week drive.

ROADS FOR NEW WHEELS: Unlike slower moving iron-rimmed wagon wheels, rubber tires spewed grit and gravel into the air, quickly wearing away macadamized roads. Something was needed to provide a more durable road surface. As early as 1810, French and English road builders began experimenting with natural tars and various cements mixed with stones and pebbles. Then, in 1824, Joseph Aspdin concocted "Portland cement" by burning a mixture of clay and lime. Aspdin had rediscovered the art of making cement, which was known to the Romans. In 1865, the mixture was first used to pave a road in Scotland. Its hard, waterproof surface made an ideal paving material and became a forerunner of the modern concrete highway.

Meanwhile, in 1837, it was found that natural asphalt could be powdered when it was heated, and then the powder could be compacted by roller into a smooth, watertight pavement. A year later, two French engineers invented a heavy steamroller.

In the United States, asphalt came into use in 1877, when Amzi Lorenzo Barber acquired the rights to extract pitch from a huge black lake in the West Indies. Soon Barber acquired a contract to pave Pennsylvania Avenue, which was then a rutted, dusty boulevard in the nation's capital. So successful was this experiment that by the late 19th century Barber's Trinidad Asphalt Company had paved the streets of several U.S. cities, including Buffalo, Chicago, New York, and San Francisco.

Building equipment kept pace with the spread of roads, evolving from primitive horse- or mule-drawn scrapers in the late 19th century to today's giant, diesel-driven earthmovers and paving machines, which can lay down a ribbon of asphalt or concrete at a rate of 30 feet or so a minute.

New York's Bronx River Parkway, the forerunner of the limited-access expressway, was opened in 1923, followed by a parkway system in nearby Westchester County and another on Long Island. Germany and Italy, too, began their respective autobahn and autostrada systems during the 1920s.

By the end of World War II, it was becoming apparent that most of America's roads and streets were inadequate for the demands of modern traffic. Many roads were underdesigned and obsolete—too curvy, too narrow, and too weak for the sizable loads they needed to convey. Bridges weren't sturdy enough; tunnels and overpasses were too low to accommodate taller vehicles.

A massive interstate highway-building program was begun in the mid-1950s. Now nearing completion, it will link every major urban center in the United States in a 50,000-mile network of multilane, divided, high-capacity highways—a project as ambitious as that started by Appius Claudius, builder of Rome's Appian Way, more than 2,000 years ago. ■

Top: **A motorist stops to pay a toll on the Pennsylvania Turnpike—America's first superhighway, which opened to traffic in October 1940.**

Opposite: **The Trans-Canada Highway winds its way through Rogers Pass in British Columbia.**

Opposite: France's Languedoc Canal, opened in 1681, extends nearly 150 miles between Toulouse and the Mediterranean Sea.

Waterways

FOR THOUSANDS OF YEARS, one of the greatest engineering challenges has been to bring water where it is needed, whether to irrigate crops or create shipping routes. During the Renaissance in Europe—and much earlier in China, Mesopotamia, and Egypt—builders cut channels through the land and erected dams to hold water. The Romans built bridge-like aqueducts. Canal locks were probably invented by the Dutch in the 14th century, enabling vessels to cross hills and detour around waterfalls and other obstacles.

By the mid-19th century, European canal engineers were slicing through land barriers, shortening world shipping lanes; the Suez Canal still serves as a maritime shortcut. Today, the St. Lawrence Seaway draws ocean-going ships into the heart of North America, offering economical transport for commodities. Over the years people have learned to harness gravity to move water and goods. They have also learned to overcome gravity with lifting devices that range from ancient water-wheels to modern hydraulic pumps that can sluice thousands of gallons a minute. ■

Rome's multilevel aqueducts carry water to the imperial city.

SOARING 120 FEET above the River Dee in Wales, Pontcysyllte Aqueduct stands as the single most impressive monument to the skill and daring of late 18th-century British canal builders. Erected by Thomas Telford, a young Scottish engineer, and by William Jessop, chief engineer on the Ellesmere Canal, the aqueduct used a trough of cast iron, rather than heavy masonry, to form its bed. Iron's much lighter weight enabled Telford to carry the aqueduct on 18 masonry piers that were much more slender than would otherwise have been possible. Springing from steep embankments, Pontcysyllte Aqueduct reflects Telford's passion for "adventurous structures" and still gives modern canal cruisers *(below)* a thrill as they drift above the valley.

CANALS AND AQUEDUCTS: Britain's industrial revolution got a boost the day the Duke of Bridgewater engaged James Brindley to build a canal leading from his lordship's coal mines at Worsley to the rapidly growing factory town of Manchester. Opened in 1761, the Bridgewater Canal halved the price of Manchester coal and gave the town a head start toward becoming England's premier industrial center. A spate of canal building followed and continued until the middle of the 19th century.

Britain's hilly terrain presented special problems. Locks—canal enclosures with gates at either end to raise or lower water levels—could stair-step hills, but builders at first avoided them because they were costly to build. Brindley himself designed aqueducts to cross rivers and valleys, as well as high, solid embankments to carry his canals across dips and swales.

By the early 1800s interlocking canals carried raw materials to burgeoning factories and finished goods to market. Scottish engineer Thomas Telford was completing the 103-mile Ellesmere Canal in western England and Wales; and the Grand Trunk, a network built at the urging of potter Josiah Wedgwood, linked the industrial Midlands with major seaports.

Along with the need to bring goods to port, growing urban populations spurred the need for adequate municipal water. The Romans had gone to great lengths to ensure that every citizen had access to water, whether collected from a local fountain or piped directly to a villa. The Roman system of aqueducts was unrivaled until the 19th century, when western cities began to be supplied with water on a comparable scale. ∎

Opposite: Curving through farmland near Napton on the Hill, a section of the Oxford Canal has changed little since the 18th century.

THE GRAND CANAL: Most of China's major rivers run from west to east. As early as the fourth century B.C., Chinese rulers realized that if they built north-south canals to link the river systems, they could unify a vast empire and ensure a steady supply of grain from the agricultural south to their northern urban centers.

In stages, a great waterway grew across China, built by multitudes of peasants. Under the harsh rule of early seventh-century A.D. Sui emperors, 5.5 million laborers are said to have worked six years to construct a 1,500-mile-long section of the canal between the port of Hangzhou and the capital at Luoyang. By later in the seventh century, the Tang and Northern Song dynasties were moving more than 300,000 tons of grain, along with paper and luxury goods, north on barges each year, over a waterway system known as the Grand Canal.

One of the first true summit canals, the Grand Canal follows the land's contours. Though the terrain is mostly flat, a slight gradient accumulates over its length; to avoid undesirable currents, stone and

Above: Heavy traffic on 40-yard-wide stretches, such as this one in Suzhou, forces barges to line up end to end—and, often, side by side.

Opposite: A Chinese dragon of barges weaves along the Grand Canal near the ancient city of Suzhou, which became rich from canalborne commerce.

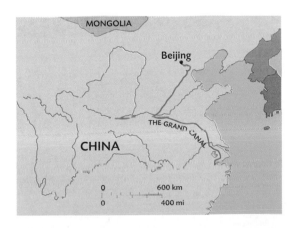

timber weirs were placed every three miles. Feeder canals drew water from distant rivers into reservoirs, and sluice gates regulated water levels. One hilly stretch required 60 gates. Where a rise proved too abrupt, boats were hauled up slipways.

Parts of the canal have remained navigable for 2,000 years. Repaired and redredged by Kublai Khan in the 13th century and by the People's Republic in the late 20th, it still serves as a route for local commerce. ■

Left. Built to carry grain and other commodities from the south to the northern capitals, the canal still moves goods through eastern China.

THE ERIE CANAL: A New York surveyor first proposed construction of a canal from the Hudson River to Lake Erie in 1724. Almost a century later, work on the 363-mile waterway began in summer 1817.

Eight years later, the canal had become navigable between Albany and Buffalo and began to shape the nation. People and goods could move easily through the Appalachians into the Great Lakes on barges hauled by horses and mules traveling on narrow towpaths. New York City had become the country's foremost port, and canalside towns quickly prospered.

Canal engineers trained on the job. They faced huge hurdles: the 419-foot drop between Utica and the Hudson to the east and the 60-foot climb up the Niagara Escarpment to the west. They gained experience on the relatively flat middle section between the Seneca River and Utica, a segment with virgin forest, demanding ingenuity. They invented a crank-and-roller device that tore down trees, and another that cleared up to 40 stumps daily. After the middle section opened, work began on the ends. In the east, the descent to Albany was challenge enough, but 86 miles had to cross the Mohawk River Valley, requiring locks and aqueducts and lining parts of the river with masonry.

The dramatic western section was last: Workers blasted away 1.5 million cubic yards of rock to build five stair-stepping double locks. Amid great fanfare, the canal was inaugurated in 1825, as a cask of Lake Erie water was emptied into the Atlantic Ocean. ■

Right, top: **Climbing 169 feet up from the Hudson River near Waterford, the Erie Canal skirts Cohoes Falls as it begins a westward swing.**

Right, below: **Parts of it restored today, the canal extends 348 miles and has 34 locks; the original canal had 83 locks and spanned 363 miles.**

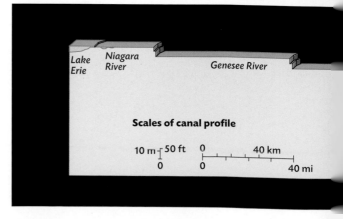

Lake Erie · Niagara River · Genesee River

Scales of canal profile

10 m ⌐ 50 ft   0   40 km
0   0   40 mi

Cross
Lake

Oneida
Lake

Hudson
River

THE SUEZ CANAL: At the 1869 opening of Egypt's Suez Canal, European heads of state, crown princes, and celebrities, hosted by dignitaries from the Ottoman Empire, sail the passage. On the banks, *fellahin* watch the celebration.

Water has often provided the most economical and efficient way to transport bulky, nonperishable goods, although it wasn't until the 18th century and the industrial revolution that canal building came into its own. Locks, inclined planes, and water lifts grew increasingly sophisticated, enabling boats and barges to travel over uneven terrain. The French canal promoter Ferdinand de Lesseps spearheaded construction of the Suez Canal and began the Panama Canal in 1882.

THE PANAMA CANAL: When the Panama Canal opened in 1914, it cut 9,000 miles from a sea voyage between New York and San Francisco. But the long-sought goal of linking the Atlantic and Pacific Oceans took more than 30 years, thousands of lives, and 387 million dollars, and it ultimately depended on controlling the anopheles mosquito.

In 1882, Ferdinand de Lesseps, the French engineer who had built the Suez Canal, began digging in Panama. Nine years later he had lost some 20,000 workers to tropical diseases and was bankrupt. In 1903, President Theodore Roosevelt secured the rights to finish the canal. Aware that doctors had pinpointed the mosquito as a transmitter of yellow fever and malaria, the U.S. Army began an eradication program that practically eliminated the disease-carrying mosquitoes by 1906.

Rather than follow the French plan to cut through the isthmus at sea level, American engineers designed locks to raise and then lower the waterway 85 feet. The move meant far less digging. Crews diverted the turbulent Chagres River to create a lake at Gatun, near the Caribbean Sea. Finally, in 1909, they began work on the locks—three at each end—each measuring 110 by 1,000 feet, with thick concrete walls and floors to hold the water.

As tall as buildings, the locks work smoothly. At the touch of a switch, the chambers drain or fill with water. The gates are also a triumph: Each 65-foot-wide, 7-foot-thick hollow leaf floats. They close to form a flat toned "V" pointed into the force of the water; its pressure stabilizes and keeps them from leaking. ■

A cruise through Panama between the Caribbean Sea and Pacific Ocean avoids a trip around South America and the winds of Cape Horn.

SEGOVIA AQUEDUCT: Majestic arches of Segovia's Roman aqueduct still rise into the Spanish sky. Throughout their empire, Roman engineers built aqueducts, equating civilization with water.

The ancient Romans demanded plentiful water for baths, fountains, and gardens—more than had ever been required before. Roman engineers developed a true municipal water supply system, so efficient that modern cities still look to it as a model. Arcades, bridges, siphons, conduits, tunnels, reservoirs, distribution pipes, and water meters formed a network that by A.D. 100 supplied 400 million gallons daily to the imperial city.

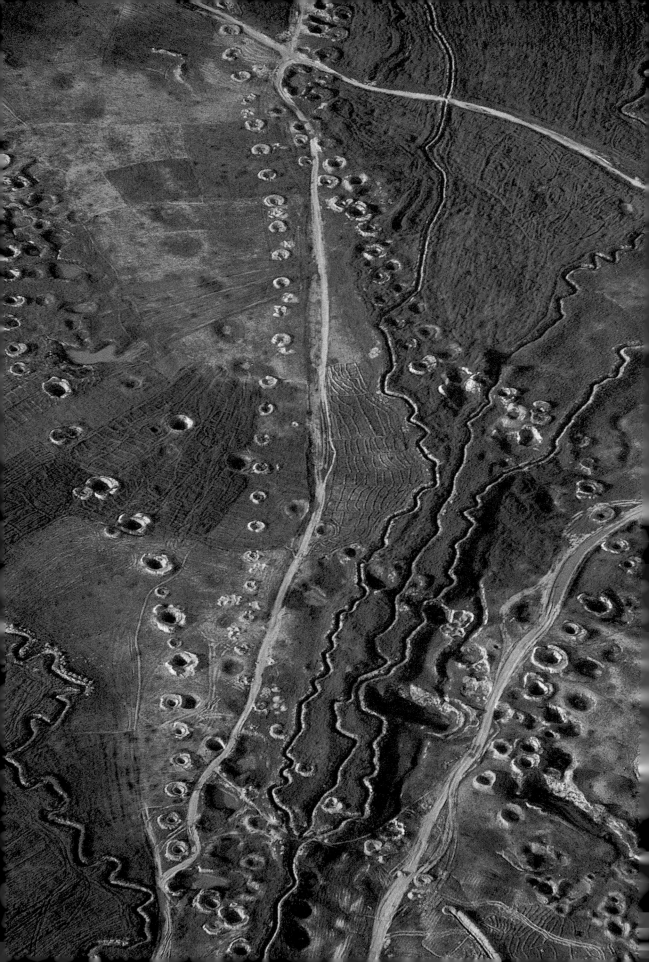

WATER SUPPLY SYSTEMS: Hydraulic engi-

neering got its start as soon as people began to farm the deserts of the ancient Middle East. In Mesopotamia, a vast system of irrigation channels brought water from the Tigris and Euphrates Rivers to the fields. Building and maintaining the system marked one of the earliest ventures in civil engineering. Large catch basins in Egypt stored floodwaters from the Nile and distributed them by a system of dikes and canals.

For more than 2,000 years, an ingenious underground system of *qanats* throughout the Middle East has used gravity to transport irrigation water. A qanat consists of a sloping tunnel driven into a hillside water table. Well-spaced vertical shafts provide outlets for tunneling headroom, as well as access and ventilation. This system provides extensive water transport without evaporation. A range of ancient devices to lift water still

Opposite: **Pockmarks in the desert indicate the paths of qanats leading to Firuzabad, Iran.**

Below: **Manholes allow access for maintenance of the sloping underground water channel via a vertical shaft. Drilled down to the water table in faraway hills, most qanats carry an average of 100,000 gallons of water daily to Iranian towns and fields.**

serves the region's farmers. Egyptians use the *shaduf,* a counterweighted lever that lifts buckets—seen in murals from 2500 B.C.—and the Archimedes' screw, invented around 250 B.C. Both are about as efficient as a small diesel-driven pump. The *noria,* a large waterwheel studded with pots, lifts water from stream to aqueduct. The *saqiya,* a refinement developed by Muslim mechanical engineers during the Middle Ages, is a more elaborate geared version driven by oxen or a waterwheel that lifts a revolving chain of pots. The aqueducts carried the water to towns or garden fountains. ■

Top: **Under the gaze of 12th-century Muslim sidewalk superintendents, a *saqiya* lifts water pots from river to aqueduct. Here, a waterwheel—not the whimsical wooden ox—drives a shaft; gears at the top turn another wheel that operates the conveyor chain of pots.**

Bridges

THE FIRST CHALLENGE TO BRIDGE BUILDERS is geography: a valley, river, bay, or other barrier. Engineers consider not only the length of span necessary but also the winds, temperature, and traffic. After site analysis, there are usually five choices of bridge type: beam, arch, suspension, cantilever, and cable-stayed. The loads on each type of bridge—deadweight and the weight of traffic—are shown in the diagram below with arrows.

The beam bridge is a simple span supported at either end. Material strength limits span length, but other spans supported on piers may be added. The arch converts vertical loads into axial compression forces that are carried into the ground. In the suspension and cable-stayed bridges, cables at both ends direct the load to towers and foundation. The suspension bridge, relatively light and flexible, can leap distances at a bound; cables anchored at either end bring the roadway loads to towers, which carry them to foundations. In the cantilever bridge, two arms extend from opposite supports, each fixed at one end. In a cable-stayed bridge, cables connect the roadway directly to a tower, which carries the load to the foundations. ■

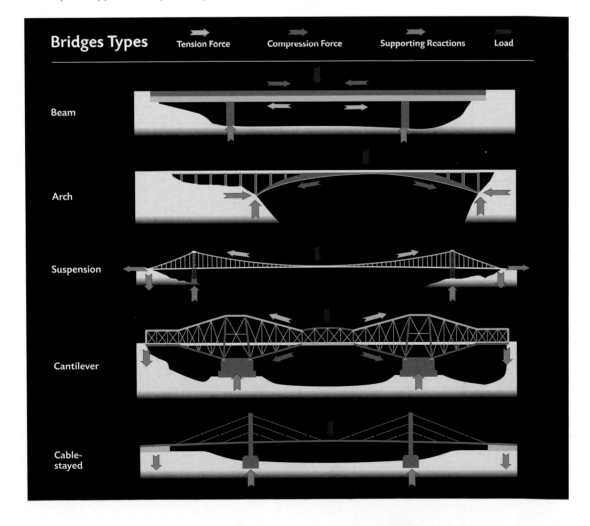

Bridges Types   Tension Force   Compression Force   Supporting Reactions   Load

Beam

Arch

Suspension

Cantilever

Cable-stayed

BEAM: Drop a tree across a stream or place a stone slab across a ditch, and you have the essence of the beam bridge—a horizontal span supported at each end. Materials have changed over time, but not the basic structure. Although the origins of such bridges are lost to antiquity, examples of them remain worldwide.

In England, stone "clapper" bridges, some dating to Celtic times, cross streams on the Devon moors. In China, the ancient An Ping Bridge carries villagers nearly a mile across an estuary along the southern coast. To place the granite beams, some weighing 100 tons, builders had to float them into position during the highest tides of spring and fall.

The advent of inexpensive cast iron and wrought iron and the rapid spread of railroads in the mid-1800s gave rise to a golden age of bridge building: Heavily laden trains could negotiate only gentle inclines, requiring their routes to be as flat as possible. This led to long viaducts, often with wide spans and high supporting towers. Truss bridges became popular because they could span long distances with relatively little material. Iron and then steel trusses soon replaced the wooden trestles that carried rails. Trusses are like beams in which thin, vertical posts and diagonals make up the area between the top and bottom horizontal members.

The Britannia Railway Bridge, a giant rectangular iron tubular beam, built in 1850, was a precursor of the modern box-girder bridge, so called because its hollow cross section acts like a beam.

Today, reinforced and prestressed concrete—both developed since the late 1800s—are widely used in beam bridge construction. ■

Opposite: **The Chesapeake Bay Bridge-Tunnel, which was completed in 1964, carries the elevated part of its two-lane roadway on some 3,000 pilings constructed from prestressed concrete.**

The modern Quesnell Bridge, above, in Alberta, Canada, contrasts with China's 12th-century An Ping Bridge, below. Although steel and concrete support the one and granite the other, both adhere to simple beam bridge principles. The An Ping Bridge's piers are shaped to withstand the assault of tides.

Above: **Rare survivor of the cast-iron bridge-building era, Ironbridge, on England's Severn River, weighs 378 tons and took only three months to assemble in 1779.**

ARCH: The Romans regarded bridge building as a sacred calling, to be entrusted to a priestly class headed by a Pontifex Maximus. They were not the first to erect arch bridges, however; the Mesopotamians had built them some 2,000 years before. The Roman arch was semicircular and so carefully crafted that its own weight held it together without mortar. A temporary wooden frame supported the arch until the keystone was added, locking the structure together. But such bridges had relatively narrow archways, which hiinder navigation.

Half a world away, a builder named Li Chun solved the problem around A.D. 610 by flattening out his arch to build the Great Stone Bridge across the Jiao River in northern China. Such flattened arches made longer bridge spans possible.

Medieval Europeans also used stone arches in bridge construction. London Bridge, one of a succession of spans that have occupied the site since ancient Roman times, crossed the River Thames on 19 arches.

The industrial revolution of the 18th and 19th centuries brought iron—both cast and wrought—to bridge building. Ironbridge, erected by Abraham Darby in 1779, spans the Severn River near Coalbrookdale, an early ironmaking center. The bridge emulates in cast iron the principles of carpentry. No bolts or rivets originally held Ironbridge together; its joints and fastenings were metal equivalents of the slots, dovetails, and mortise-and-tenon grooves used by woodworkers. When a flood in 1795 demolished most of the Severn's wood bridges, Ironbridge stood fast, allowing water to pass through and demonstrating the strength and durability of iron. ■

Opposite: **Encrusted with houses and shops, Old London Bridge stood for some 600 years. Begun in 1176, the bridge took 33 years to build across the 900-foot-wide River Thames, which reportedly was diverted four miles during construction.**

Above: **Rising through the mist, the Golden Gate Bridge spans San Francisco Bay in a 4,200-foot stride. Finished in 1937, it has the tallest towers of any bridge.**

SUSPENSION: Unsurpassed in length of span, the suspension bridge arcs gracefully across empty space to connect distant or hard-to-reach places. Major spans can vault more than a mile.

Four elements distinguish a modern suspension bridge: its roadway, also called the deck, which usually stretches over the main span and the two side spans; towers at both ends of the main span; cables slung over the tops of the towers; and solid anchorages, normally at the ends of the side spans. From the main cables hang vertical supports called suspenders, or

hangers, which carry the weight of the deck and its live load up to the cables. On some bridges, saddles on top of the towers allow the cables to adjust to temperature changes and shifts in load.

Anchorage blocks, constructions of steel and reinforced concrete, hold the cable ends in place. The weight of these anchorages resists the pull of the cables. Trusses beneath the roadway stiffen the deck. ■

Opposite: **A bridge of braided grass crosses a gorge in Peru, recalling Inca spans that once laced such ravines.**

Above: **A snapping cable claims two lives in this contemporary lithograph.**

THE BROOKLYN BRIDGE: The Brooklyn Bridge, in its day the world's longest suspension span, crosses New York's East River, linking Manhattan and Brooklyn. Designed by John Roebling, an immigrant engineer and creative genius, the bridge took 14 years to build—at a cost of 15 million dollars and at least 20 lives, Roebling's included. His son, Washington, finished the task. The bridge deck arcs 1,595 feet between towers that rise 276 feet above the river. Side spans, each 930 feet long, reach from tower to shore.

Hailed as the eighth wonder of the world when finished in 1883, the Brooklyn Bridge required prodigious engineering. To sink piers for the massive granite towers, Washington Roebling used the pneumatic caisson technique, a recent European invention. In two airtight timber boxes, workers dug down almost to bedrock. The boxes were then filled with concrete.

Laborers digging inside the caissons worked in air pressurized to keep water from entering. More than a hundred workers were stricken with the bends because its cause and prevention (by use of decompression chambers) were not well understood. The bridge's four main suspension cables used steel wire—nearly 15,000 miles of it. The bridge united two rival and independent cities, helping to establish the metropolis of New York City. ■

Opposite: **Gothic towers webbed with steel soar 276 feet above New York's East River.**

Below: **Excavated from below and weighted on top by huge blocks of granite, a timber caisson inches downward toward bedrock.**

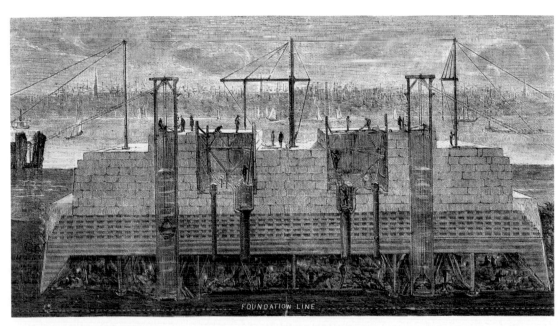

FOUNDATION LINE

Above: Ganter Bridge, which opened in 1980, traverses a Swiss Alpine valley. The bridge combines both cantilevers and cable stays for strength and grace.

CANTILEVER: In a cantilever bridge, two beams project from opposite piers. Each beam is supported by its pier and anchored at one end, like a swimming pool diving board. In such a bridge, the projecting beams may meet in the middle, forming a rigid, continuous beam. Some cantilevers have projecting spans that support a shorter, central span. Such is the case with Scotland's Forth Bridge *(opposite)*. Cantilever bridges are generally stiffer than suspension bridges and hence suitable for heavy traffic, such as a railroad train with its rhythmic, pounding thrust.

Designed by Benjamin Baker and completed in 1890, the massive mile-long Forth Bridge *(opposite)* near Edinburgh was an engineering triumph of its time—one of the first major railroad bridges to use steel and, until the opening of the Quebec Bridge in 1918, the world's longest span.

On three massive piers, cantilevers form two main spans, each 1,710 feet long, about 150 feet above the water. The steelwork includes more than 50,000 tons of tubes and girders. But such bridges are expensive to

build and maintain. The dawn of the automobile age and the development of reinforced concrete ushered in a new era of bridge building. Here was an inexpensive, strong material that required little upkeep.

In the 1900s, engineers continued to experiment with new materials and techniques. With the Ganter Bridge *(above)*, a hybrid form was introduced in 1980 by Swiss engineer Christian Menn. Here cantilever spans supporting the midsection are themselves supported by cable stays embedded in prestressed concrete. The concrete walls add safety and shield the cables from stress and corrosion. Menn's main motive, however, was aesthetic: Like a sculptured bird, the Ganter Bridge appears to take wing. ■

Opposite, top: Tubes big enough for a train to roll through strengthen the massive towers of Scotland's Forth Bridge, a triumph of steel design. The steelwork includes more than 50,000 tons of tubes and girders.

Opposite, bottom: Three caissons *(not shown)* embedded in the river and filled with concrete support the towers.

CABLE-STAYED: Its towers connected directly to the deck by steel cables, the cable-stayed bridge represents a modification of a technique long used to strengthen suspension bridges. John Roebling included cable stays in his design for the Brooklyn Bridge, along with vertical suspenders.

Cable-stayed bridges are popular for medium-length bridges because they do not require the large anchorages of suspension bridges and because they can be economically built by the cantilever method. The diagonal steel cables called stays attach the decks—often box-girder structures of prestressed concrete—to the tall towers or masts.

German engineers pioneered the design of cable-stayed bridges in the 1950s and 1960s, especially for Rhine River crossings destroyed during World War II. Particularly impressive is a series of light, harp-type bridges with parallel cables built as a family at the bend in the Rhine River at Dusseldorf.

In the United States, a noteworthy cable-stayed bridge was finished in 1987 across Florida's Tampa Bay. The 4.1-mile Sunshine Skyway Bridge carries four traffic lanes on a divided road that sweeps 175 feet above the main channel. The bridge's precast, prestressed roadway sits atop massive twin piers 175 feet high, 8 other main span piers, and 36 approach piers.

In southern France, the Millau Viaduct became the tallest cable-stayed bridge on completion in 2004. Spanning the Tarn River Valley, it stands 1,118 feet high at its loftiest point. It broke three world records: highest pylons, highest mast, and highest road bridge deck. ∎

Taller even than the Eiffel Tower, the Millau Viaduct was designed and built by a French-British team that aimed to give it "the delicacy of a butterfly." Of his design, the world-renowned architect Norman Foster said, "A work of man must fuse with nature. "

Opposite: A 19-mile rock causeway carries the Southern Pacific Railroad across Utah's Great Salt Lake.

Railroads

Above: Two engines pull a Denver and Rio Grande train up Colorado's San Juan Mountains in a photograph from the 1880s. A decade and a half earlier, Swedish chemist Alfred Nobel had invented dynamite, making ledge blasting easier and safer than with earlier explosives.

ON THE TRANS-AUSTRALIAN RAILWAY, trains crossing the treeless Nullarbor Plain shoot across the world's largest stretch of straight track: 300 miles without a single curve. But few locations on Earth offer the long, flat, straight stretches that permit locomotives to pull heavy loads at top speeds. The challenge to the railroad engineer has been, from the first rail lines in the 1820s and 1830s, to reduce the factors that slow trains down—grades and curves—by flattening and straightening the roadbed. Railroads work best with grades no steeper than 2 percent; tunnels, bridges, and landfill all help keep grades to a minimum.

Engineers also seek to avoid grade crossings—intersections with highways or other railroad tracks—that force trains to slow down. And engineers the world over have had to find ways to go around, over, or through forests, swamps, mountains, rivers, and deep valleys.

Locating the line is crucial. A well-chosen route might bring in great profits; a badly planned road could lead to financial ruin. Land that looks easy can still present serious problems. The locating engineers—route surveyors sent to examine the terrain and choose a route—would balance difficulty of construction and cost against safety, efficiency, and operating expenses as they pounded in the stakes marking the line. ■

THE TRANSCONTINENTAL: Perhaps no other engineering feat thrilled 19th-century Americans as much as the building of the 2,000-mile transcontinental railroad. Surely no other enterprise overcame such physical and logistical nightmares.

Rails for the Central Pacific, building east from Sacramento, had to be transported by ship around Cape Horn. The Union Pacific Railroad, starting west from Omaha, Nebraska, had to ship timbers from the East to the treeless plains at great cost; 2,400 wooden crossties for every mile of track laid also had to be brought in. Attacks by Indians meant every rail crew had to keep carbines handy.

As soon as the route was marked, grading crews began blasting and hacking away huge volumes of rock to achieve the minimal grade desired. Tracklayers were close behind.

The Central Pacific faced very severe labor shortages. When the first 50 Chinese workers demonstrated that they were both hardworking and tenacious—as well as cheap labor—thousands more were employed. Crossing the Sierra Nevada, it was the Chinese who blasted out the ledges along the steep

Below: **A throng of revelers in Promontory, Utah, toasts the inauguration of the Transcontinental Railroad in 1869.**

Above: **Cutting corners to speed tracklaying, workers often built quick, temporary trestles. A masonry bridge later replaced this one at Green River, Wyoming.**

gorges. Lowered in baskets, they drilled holes in the rock, tamped powder, set the fuses, and then yelled to be hauled up quickly.

Tunneling through the hard granite of the high Sierras was complicated by the extremely harsh winter of 1866-67. Blizzards piled drifts so deep that 12 locomotives could not push a snowplow through. Miles of snowsheds had to be designed and then constructed to protect the tracks.

Tracklaying went faster, however, in the desert, despite sweltering heat and severe water shortages. Compensated by federal loans and rewarded by land grants for every mile of track completed, the two companies persevered, passing each other near Ogden, Utah, and continuing right on building. By the time the government ordered them to join up at Promontory, some 225 miles of parallel track had been laid.

On May 10, 1869, as the final spikes—of gold— were driven and locomotives from east and west touched cowcatchers, telegraphers flashed the news across the country: "Done." ■

HIGH-SPEED TRAINS: In 1964, Japan opened a new age of high-speed rail travel with the New Tokaido Line, which ran between Tokyo and Osaka at a top speed of 131 miles per hour. Today, the "bullet train" is a broad network of rail lines running throughout Japan's main island. It requires a specially designed roadbed—flat, straight, raised above all grade crossings—that carries the tracks through urban areas containing 40 percent of Japan's people and 70 percent of its industry. Modern railroad engineering serves notice: Ideal conditions—flat, straight, no crossings—can be created virtually anywhere.

Opposite: The Trans-Arabian Pipeline, completed in 1950, stretches 1,068 miles between the Persian Gulf and the Mediterranean Sea.

Pipelines

SELDOM SEEN, pipelines are crucial to a modern industrial world. Underground conduits have irrigated the Middle East for millennia, and a gravity-fed water system supplied ancient Rome. As long ago as 1580, primitive pumps distributed piped water in London. By the mid-1800s, U.S. water lines were widespread.

America's first oil pipeline was only two inches in diameter. Built in 1865 by Samuel Van Syckel, it carried the equivalent of 800 barrels a day from a field in Titusville, Pennsylvania, to a railroad five miles away.

Since then, engineers have worked to build pipelines of increasing diameter and length. Steel pipes, and the introduction of electric arc welding in the 1920s, helped usher in modern pipelaying. Advances in technology made it possible to move oil cheaply and quickly at pressures of up to 2,000 pounds per square inch. Today, a mostly subterranean network extends some 2.5 million miles across North America, carrying natural gas or petroleum from supplier to consumer. ■

WORKERS DIG TRENCHES and prepare the "Big Inch" for burial as part of a World War II project to ensure northern U.S. factories adequate fuel. Measuring 24 inches in diameter, "Big Inch" carried crude petroleum 1,341 miles between Longview, Texas, and central Pennsylvania. Extensions of the pipeline fed refineries in Philadelphia, New Jersey, and other industrial centers. A smaller pipeline, 20-inch "Little Big Inch," ran parallel and carried refined petroleum products such as heating oil and gasoline. Between them, the two pipelines carried about half a million barrels a day.

Above: **Welders work on a feeder line near Prudhoe Bay.**

THE TRANS-ALASKA: When the magnitude of the Prudhoe Bay discovery became known in June 1968, oilworkers dubbed it an "elephant field," and geologists said it was "one of the largest petroleum accumulations known to the world today."

Prudhoe Bay, where Alaska's North Slope meets the frigid waters of the Arctic Ocean, is one of the most hostile environments on Earth. Here, far above the Arctic Circle, winter winds howl and temperatures can hover around minus 60°F. During the brief summers, the permafrost thaws just enough to become a tractor-swallowing quagmire and breeding grounds for some of the world's bloodthirstiest insects.

Add to that the fact that the pipeline had to scale three mountain ranges, cross more than 350 rivers and streams, and traverse zones of intense seismic activity—

Opposite: **An elevated section of the Trans-Alaska Pipeline crosses the tundra. Made in Japan, the 48-inch pipeline can carry up to 2.1 million barrels of oil a day.**

Below: **Spanning Alaska's girth, the Trans-Alaska Pipeline traces an 800-mile route between Prudhoe Bay and the southern terminus at the Port of Valdez.**

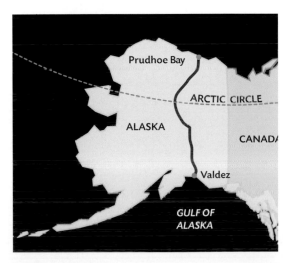

as well as overcome environmental and political concerns—and the task became gargantuan. Getting off the ground on the three-year, eight-billion-dollar project took an oil embargo and a 1973 act of Congress.

For more than half its route, the pipeline is elevated on what is called the "high-rise ditch." This prevents oil heated by friction to about 125°F from warming the pipe and melting the permafrost. The elevated portions are cradled by tubular supports placed in the ground and refrigerated to avoid thawing the permafrost. Teflon-coated "shoes" allow the pipe to slide freely within the supports, which is necessary to accommodate the widely fluctuating temperatures.

Where the pipeline crosses caribou migration routes, it goes underground. Insulation and a system of small, separate lines carrying refrigerated brine keep the ground around the pipe frozen. Engineers designed special gate valves at river crossings and other sensitive areas to automatically stop the oil flow if the pipe ruptures. When crossing streams and rivers, the pipeline was buried and weighted down with special nine-ton concrete jackets. On 13 crossings, including the 2,300-foot-wide Yukon River, bridges were built to carry the pipe. Since its 1977 completion, the pipeline has carried more than 15 billion barrels of oil to Valdez. ∎

2: HEIGHT

AND DEPTH

Towers
Tunnels
Skyscrapers

THE REMARKABLE FEATS OF CONSTRUCTION of the past 200 years were made possible by an industrial revolution. New methods of ironmaking gave engineers a building material stronger than wood and stone. New iron railways and bridges and iron buildings such as the Crystal Palace of 1851 made use of prefabricated pieces, as did Gustave Eiffel in building his landmark 1889 tower in Paris.

In the later 19th century, advances in making steel from iron enabled William Le Baron Jenney and other engineers in Chicago to erect the first skyscrapers, which the elevator of Elisha Otis made practical to use. Concrete reinforced with steel opened further possibilities in construction. As the new materials made possible new works, structural engineering emerged as a profession, and engineers proved that the new structural forms could be elegant as well as efficient.

After World War II, engineers applied a growing knowledge of structural mechanics to develop internal frames and bracing so strong that whole buildings could be covered in glass. In the 1970s and 1980s, rigid-tube construction was introduced, which enabled buildings to rise 100 stories and more.

Computer technology spurred another revolution. Computers can generate theoretical structures for analysis. Some computer programs analyze gravity forces, while others calculate the impact of wind shear on scale models in wind tunnels or gauge the impact of earthquake shock. Increasingly, working robots and automated machinery are playing a role in construction.

The computer revolution also affected tunnel building. Channel Tunnel engineers used a computer and laser system, aided by four Navstar satellites, to monitor the tunnel ends continually during excavation. Whenever the tunnel inched off course, the computer automatically signaled a course correction to hydraulic jacks, which in turn adjusted the excavation machinery.

Clues to the future of skyscrapers may lie in such structures as Hong Kong's Bank of China. It blends steel and concrete in an innovative way, creating an economical design that is rigid yet light. Instead of using the standard internal steel frame, engineers employed a space-frame design of 3-D trussing. Perhaps Frank Lloyd Wright's dream of a "mile-high" skyscraper may yet be realized. ■

Preceding pages: Looking east across Shanghai's Huangpu River toward the new financial center of Pudong. The Oriental Pearl television tower at left dominates the skyline.

Left: Weighing some 450 tons, the first of five tunneling machines bores the Channel Tunnel, connecting England to the European mainland.

Towers

FOR CENTURIES, TOWERS HAVE EXERTED a powerful, often spiritual, influence on those who view them. In the Bible, the Tower of Babel symbolized mankind's audacity and presumed self-sufficiency. When it rose too close to heaven, God struck it down.

Early masonry towers were built for military or religious purposes; medieval bell towers, such as Venice's St. Mark's, are notable examples. Lighthouses were also early masonry tower forms; the ancient Pharos of Alexandria stood in the Mediterranean until 1326.

Tower building changed dramatically during the industrial revolution. Strong building materials, such as iron, became available, enabling builders to push structures higher into the sky. New concepts in designing foundations and prefabricating sections were among a number of engineering innovations. No longer in service of religion or war, towers became symbolic of technological progress and material success. Countries across the world proudly erected towers purely as engineering feats, often as tributes to national heroes.

Since then, materials such as steel and reinforced concrete have replaced iron. Gasoline-powered cranes have superseded steam-powered ones. Beginning with the 1889 Eiffel Tower and the previous height record holder, the 1884 Washington Monument, a succession of towers has followed at least two basic engineering principles: the need for a strong foundation and a strategy to resist the destructive force of the wind.

The tilt of one of the world's most famous towers, the Leaning Tower of Pisa, arose out of a fundamental error: In laying the foundation, 12th-century Pisan builders concentrated too much weight in a small area of soft soil. Subsequently, the soil has settled unevenly under the weight of the tower, causing it to lean.

For this reason, engineers focus carefully on the tower foundation. They must often dig to bedrock, sink piles or caissons, or spread the load over a wider area. Even with a strong foundation, a tall tower can topple in a strong wind. Short masonry towers can resist the wind through the deadweight of stone. Wind has become the single greatest concern in building lighter and taller towers. For his famous tower, Gustave Eiffel designed an open latticework structure with a new form to withstand wind stress efficiently. ■

1759.

BED ROOM

LIVING ROOM OR KITCHEN

STORE ROOM

STORE ROOM

ENTRANCE

WATER

ROCK

LOW WA

JOHN SMEATON (1724-1792), England's first "civil engineer," built the Eddystone Light on a rocky islet off the coast of southwest England. Though not the first lighthouse here, Smeaton's building followed a unique design using iron-reinforced granite and waterproof cement. It lasted a record 123 years.

THE EIFFEL TOWER: From a distance, the Eiffel Tower seems poised for flight—a sleek rocket ship out of a Jules Verne novel. Up close, the lines turn into a web of intersecting girders.

The simple yet masterly 9,700-ton iron structure rises nearly 1,000 feet into the sky. Completed in 1889 to mark the centennial of the French Revolution, the Eiffel Tower soared nearly twice as high as the world's then tallest structure, the Washington Monument. A testament to French technical proficiency, it remained the world's tallest structure for 40 years.

The genius behind the tower was Gustave Eiffel, a celebrated structural engineer and bridge builder. Iron was the material of the industrial revolution, and Eiffel was a master of the medium. His revolutionary design for the tower traced the shape of the wind forces on the monument, which were greater at the base and tapered as they rose to the top. Although it was criticized at first for its unprecedented size and appearance, the Eiffel Tower soon won admiration for its elegance and has since become a symbol of modern France.

Although 19th-century engineers had extensive experience using iron in bridge building, there were few precedents for tall structures. But Eiffel had been studying tower design since the 1860s, when he began to build tall railroad viaducts through the windy valleys of Europe's Massif Central. He tackled the engineering problem with a combination of mathematics, precision, and patience, employing 30 draftsmen for 18 months. Because the tower's edges were curved and the trusses and supports were graduated from top to

An archival photograph from 1888, when most of the ironwork was erected, hints at the construction process. Horse-drawn drays brought prefabricated sections to the base of the structure from Eiffel's workshop three miles away. Steam-powered cranes then hoisted the individual sections into position.

bottom, each piece was designed independently to reflect variable inclinations and to bear different loads. Time constraints and the magnitude of the project motivated Eiffel to prefabricate all the sections off-site, a novel technique.

Precision was essential because the pieces had to be riveted together and the rivet holes placed just so. Eiffel's care paid off: Even when cranes raised a section into place 164 feet up, the rivet holes matched. No amount of precision, however, could account for all the adjustments needed to erect the tower. Eiffel devised hydraulic jacks that fit inside each of the four main columns acting as the tower's legs. Using the jacks, each capable of lifting 900 tons, Eiffel could minutely adjust the angle of the main columns—a spectacular feat for the era. ■

Opposite: **Thousands of lights call attention to the elegance and structural simplicity of France's most famous landmark, the Eiffel Tower.**

GOING UP: Modern double-decked elevators carry tourists at some 2.4 feet per second up to a restaurant and an observation deck. The elevators are custom-built to move upward and downward at two different angles in order to match the angles of the tower's legs. There are elevators in each of the tower's four legs, none of which are identical; however, each is double-decked with large windows so that tourists can enjoy the view. In the basements of the eastern and western legs is hydraulic machinery built by Gustave Eiffel in 1899.

Above: **For two decades, starting in 1854, the unfinished monument stood abandoned, a bleak reminder of Civil War-era turmoil.**

THE WASHINGTON MONUMENT: With its simple, elegant lines, the Washington Monument serves as the triumphant focal point of the Mall, Washington, D.C.'s grassy promenade. Honoring George Washington, it rises 555 feet, the world's tallest obelisk.

Thomas Casey, an Army engineer known for his Civil War forts, inherited the project in 1876, after work had stalled at the 156-foot mark for two decades. Casey had first to reinforce a deficient foundation, a particular challenge because about one-quarter of the monument was already standing. Without displacing the existing foundation, he carefully removed large amounts of soil from underneath and around the foundation, immediately filling the holes with concrete. His plan used a network of iron rail tracks, derricks, concrete mixers, and hoisting equipment. Concrete

buttresses added additional support and also served to connect the old and new foundations.

Casey's upper walls are much thinner than the earlier, lower ones, reflecting his engineering skill. To place them, he devised an iron skeleton for the monument's interior to support a temporary platform elevator that hauled stonework. The skeleton also anchored four derricks that swung the masonry into place.

For the 300-ton roof, rising the last 55 feet, marble slabs up to 7 inches thick were laid on 12 vertical ribs that converged at the apex. The 3,300-pound capstone was set in 1884, five decades after the project had begun. ■

Opposite: **White marble from quarries in Maryland faces the Washington Monument, the world's tallest structure until the Eiffel Tower was built.**

THE GATEWAY ARCH: Though the arch has been a common construction feature throughout history, its use reached a zenith in 1965 with the completion of St. Louis's Gateway Arch. The nation's tallest monument, it soars 630 feet into the sky. The marvel is that it stands at all.

In 1948, Finnish-American architect Eero Saarinen won the design competition for the monument, beating 171 other entrants. But his plans to create a self-supporting stainless steel arch the size of a 60-story building were soon shown to be fatally flawed: Two individual legs that curved inward to join at the center would be unstable at such a height. More than a decade later, project engineers led by John Dinkeloo, who had worked with Saarinen, devised a new engineering plan based on a single hollow, curving tube; they looked to a special building material and deep foundations to stabilize the form.

Stainless steel was chosen for its tensile strength, durability, flexibility, and beauty. The Pittsburgh–Des Moines Steel Company fabricated the sections for the arch out of 886 tons of the material, which represents more stainless steel than has been used on any other single construction project. The cost was exceptionally high.

The arch features a strong, stressed-skin design. A cross section of one of the legs reveals an equilateral triangle; each of the triangle's three sides is built from two walls of steel plate. High-strength steel bolts connect the two plates. Concrete, bolstered by steel tensioning rods, fills the space between the plates. By tightening the bolts and rods, the steel skin was stretched tight.

Each leg tapers from 54 feet on a side at ground level to 17 feet at the apex. The resulting structure supports itself.

Looking west, the 630-foot-high arch frames much of downtown St. Louis, above. Although it was originally conceived as two separate legs, the arch was eventually constructed as a single hollow, curving tube of stainless steel, opposite.

The construction team lifted the first six steel sections into place with standard ground-based cranes. After that, two special cranes placed on mobile derricks ("creeper cranes") were used. As work progressed, each crane climbed higher on a track system attached directly to the leg. When each section of the arch was raised, it was bolted into place. On October 28, 1965, as jacks pushed the two legs apart and hundreds of people watched, workers dropped the keystone section into place. The creeper cranes then backed down the legs, taking up their tracks as they went. ∎

THE TALLEST TOWERS: If the Eiffel Tower looks like a 19th-century rocket ship, then Toronto's CN Tower represents a spaceship of the future. The tallest freestanding structure in the world, the CN Tower rises like a needle 1,815 feet above the city.

Completed in 1975, the CN Tower was constructed by Canadian National Railways to improve television reception in the area. Gently tapering as it rises, the tower is made of prestressed concrete and reinforced steel. Its narrow profile is deceptive: The tower is so strong that 120-mile-an-hour winds would create a barely discernible wobble at the level of the Skypod, a seven-story barrel-like ring about 1,000 feet aboveground.

Construction took just 40 months, thanks to the ingenious use of a technique that, though long established, had never been attempted on this scale. Mixed on-site, special high-quality concrete was poured into a massive mold, called a slip form, attached to the base. As the concrete hardened, a ring of climbing hydraulic jacks moved the slip form higher. With this technique, the tower rose some 20 feet a day. A helicopter mounted the 335-foot steel transmission mast by airlifting the 39 mast sections into place. Workers excavated more than 62,000 tons of earth for the structure's massive foundation, which rests on a shale bed 50 feet belowground.

Glass-fronted elevators can whisk tourists to the Skypod at a speed of 20 feet per second. Special sensors reduce the speed of the elevators during heavy winds. ■

Left: **Still under construction at press time, Dubai's Burj Tower surpassed the CN Tower in height in fall 2007.**

Opposite: **A futuristic symbol of the television age, the CN Tower pierces the Toronto sky. Broadcast antennas on the transmission mast are protected from ice buildup by 270 fiberglass panels.**

985 Feet

890 Feet

Statfjord B Oil Platform

Eiffel Tower

THE STATFJORD B: Capable of withstanding 100-foot waves and the punishing winds of the North Sea, the 890-foot-high Statfjord B Oil and Gas Platform accommodates 204 people and stores two million barrels of oil, as well as the equipment for recovering up to 250,000 barrels a day.

The Statfjord B is the heaviest movable structure ever built, relying on its 890,000-ton weight to anchor it to the seafloor in 489 feet of water. Construction workers completed the massive platform in 1981, when they joined the preassembled base and deck in a protected, deep-water Norwegian fjord. Twenty-four reinforced concrete cylinders make up the base; from four of them rise hollow concrete legs (the other 20 store crude oil). On top of the legs sits a steel deck, which holds equipment, a hotel, and a helipad. Joining the 40,000-ton deck and the base was a delicate operation requiring enormous precision.

Tugboats towed the finished platform to the Statfjord field, the world's largest offshore oil and gas field, 114 miles west of Norway. There, engineers filled Statfjord B's 20 concrete base cylinders with seawater, sinking the platform to the seafloor. A steel skirt built around the cylinders penetrated 13 feet into the floor, adding stability.

Drilling machinery operates through two of the four legs. Statfjord B's oil recovery proved such a success that it recouped the $1.8 billion construction costs for its multinational owners before celebrating its first anniversary at sea. ∎

Its 40,000-ton steel deck and base mated, the Statfjord B Platform awaits transport from a Norwegian fjord to the North Sea's Statfjord field, left. The platform's drilling rig, helipad, and living areas are clearly visible and rise almost to the height of the Eiffel Tower, inset.

Tunnels

EVER SINCE HUMANS LEARNED TO ENLARGE THE CAVE, we have found reasons to tunnel through the earth: for mining and storage, for carrying water, for sewerage and drainage, and for transportation.

A tunnel is an underground passage excavated from inside and lined for support. It may pass beneath city streets, under a riverbed or seafloor, or through the side of a mountain. In cross section, its walls can be circular, oval, or horseshoe—shapes that best withstand earth pressure. Like other large structures, tunnels rely on foundations to transfer massive loads to the earth below. Engineers determine a tunnel's form and building method by its function and the type of ground through which it will pass. Once excavated, soft ground must be reinforced; rock tunnels often also need support.

Today, soft-ground tunnels are built with giant tunnel boring machines (TBMs), which excavate, dispose of earth, and add reinforcement. ■

A diamond drill is used to bore the Mont Cenis Tunnel, the first great Alpine tunnel, completed in 1871

MOUNTAIN TUNNELS: Solid rock offers the greatest challenge to tunnel builders and their equipment, whether they are boring through a mountain or burrowing through a hillside. Piercing hard rock takes precise geological knowledge and specialized technology, both of which have evolved over time.

When test boring along a route isn't possible—as is usually so with mountain tunnels—surveyors must rely on analysis based on surface indications, plus a bit of luck. No one can know for sure the nature of the ground inside, or predict when a subterranean water pocket will burst through a fissure or when seismic forces will damage tunnel supports and explode a rock wall.

The coming of railroads in the 19th century also ushered in the great age of tunnel building. Steep grades prevented trains from traversing high mountains, so engineers had to invent ways to bore through them efficiently and safely. In fact, engineers could not anticipate the difficulties ahead, including the costs in money and human life. For centuries, engineers had used hammers and chisels or "fire setting" (the rock face was heated

and then doused with water to shatter it) to bore through rock. In the 1600s, gunpowder came into use to break rock. As late as the mid-19th century, blasting gangs still tamped black gunpowder into holes bored by handheld drills. Typically, the workers drilled blast holes using an ancient technique in which one man

Top: A steam locomotive emerges from the extravagantly arched Italian portal of the Mont Cenis, or Frejus, Tunnel.

Below: Using carriage-mounted pneumatic drills, workers advance a heading of the Hoosac Tunnel, America's first major rock tunnel, begun in 1851. Behind them, crews enlarge the tunnel with chisels.

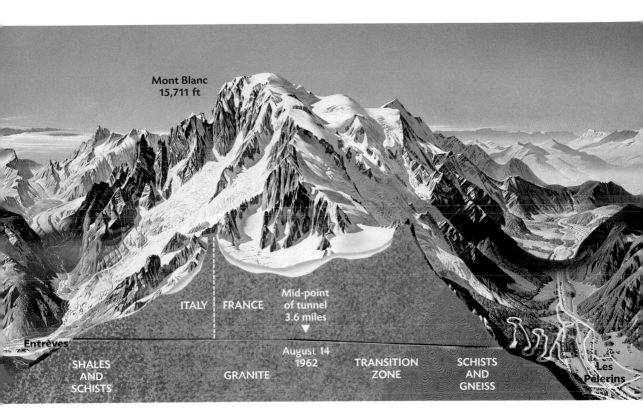

Mont Blanc
15,711 ft

ITALY | FRANCE

Mid-point
of tunnel
3.6 miles
▼

Entrèves

August 14
1962

SHALES
AND
SCHISTS

GRANITE

TRANSITION
ZONE

SCHISTS
AND
GNEISS

Les
Pèlerins

hammered a "jumper"—a steel drill with a chisel-shaped bit—while another held and turned it.

In the early 1850s, work began on an unprecedented five-mile railroad tunnel through Hoosac Mountain in Massachusetts. Initially, the old methods were used. But by the the tunnel's completion in 1875, Hoosac engineers were using the technology—mechanized drills and reliable explosives—still used today. Their first attempts involved a 70-ton, steam-driven drilling machine. A boiler plant outside the tunnel supplied the steam, which dissipated much of its energy en route to the drills, drenching the workers in steam.

In the 1860s, Germaine Sommeiller, chief engineer of the Mont Cenis Tunnel, the first such Alpine passage, introduced some major innovations. His "water-spout machine" was an efficient mechanical drill driven by hydraulically compressed air. To maneuver the machines, he invented a rail mounted, wheeled carriage that could carry up to nine rock drills and required a crew of 30. Sommeiller refused to share his design with the Hoosac builders, so engineer Charles Burleigh

One of the world's longest highway tunnels pierces Mont Blanc, western Europe's crown peak. The 31-foot-high tube offers a direct route between Paris and Rome.

devised his own, even more powerful pneumatic drill—a hybrid of the steam and compressed-air machines. Burleigh's new drill became the prototype for subsequent piston-type drills.

The year 1866 saw a breakthrough in explosives with the introduction of nitroglycerine, first used by the Hoosac's chief engineer, Thomas Doane. Dynamite, the new explosive perfected and patented by Alfred Nobel in 1867, eventually replaced nitroglycerine as the agent of choice. Three years after manufacturing began, it was used to blast a second Alpine railroad tunnel, at St. Gotthard.

Headlines were made again in 1962 with the successful boring of the 7.2-mile-long Mont Blanc Tunnel between Italy and France, completed in just three years. Since then, Switzerland has built several longer Alpine auto tunnels. ■

Honshu

Tsugaru Strait

A massive complex of three interconnected tubes forms Japan's 34-mile Seikan Tunnel, built between 1971 and 1988 and dug through exceptionally difficult rock.

UNDERWATER TUNNELS: Variations in the soft soils of riverbeds and seafloors present special challenges to engineers who build tunnels beneath the water. Whether going through silt, sand, gravel, mud, or clay, such tunnels pose an inherent risk of caving in and flooding.

Tunneling beneath the water was virtually an impossible task before the invention of the protective shield, an ingenious device inspired by the burrowing mole and the teredo, or shipworm—a marine mollusk notorious for boring passageways through submerged ship timbers.

The mechanics of the teredo's strong, protective shell-plates intrigued engineer Marc Isambard Brunel. In 1825, he employed a rudimentary tunneling shield modeled after the mollusk's. The shield made possible the construction of London's Thames Tunnel—the world's first true underwater passage.

Brunel's shield consisted of 12 cast-iron frames, each divided into three vertical floors, or cells. The frames were loosely joined, forming an 80-ton structure that contained 36 cells measuring about three by six feet each—large enough to hold a worker while he excavated. The shield fit over the tunnel face and temporarily supported it—and the tunnel walls—until the brick lining was in place. The shield was separated into three movable sections advanced by screw jacks.

Over the following decades, the procedure was greatly improved. In 1864, British engineer Peter Barlow patented a one-piece cylindrical shield and a cast-iron lining, built as the shield advanced. The shield allowed tunneling through heavy silt, clay, and mud.

A decade later, Barlow's protégé, James Henry Greathead, devised a cylindrical shield that used compressed air to resist the water. Greathead's system equalized the air pressure inside with the water pressure outside the tunnel—similar to the pneumatic caisson method used in building underwater bridge foundations. The system was introduced during construction of the City & South London Railway Tunnel in 1886. The twin circular bores measured about ten feet in diameter and marked the start of modern underwater tunneling.

Since the 1950s, sunken tubes have replaced shield and compressed air methods wherever possible. Initiated as an experiment on the Detroit River Railroad Tunnel in 1906, this procedure calls for sinking sealed, prefabricated tubing sections into a dredged trench, joining them, and then covering them with backfill. A less expensive system, it also is less risky

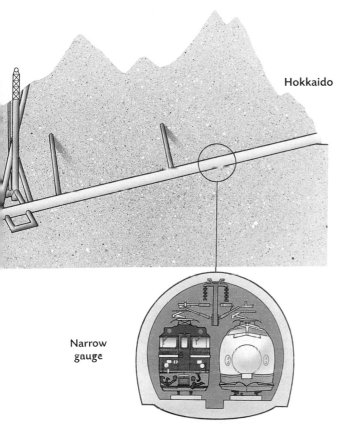

Hokkaido

Narrow
gauge

because air pressure inside the tube is the same as it is at sea level.

Advanced technology, such as laser-optical surveying and guiding techniques and giant full-area tunnel boring machines, and the use of shotcrete, or sprayed concrete, to stabilize headings and stave off flooding, have also revolutionized underwater tunneling.

Ironically, the space age has ushered in a new era of railway tunnels. Notable are Japan's 34-mile-long Seikan Tunnel, the world's longest, completed in 1988, and the Channel Tunnel between Britain and France. Too long to ventilate adequately for motor vehicles, these tunnels are designed for high-speed, nonpolluting electric trains. ■

"I AM GOING INTO TUNNEL WORK," Clifford M. Holland solemnly vowed to a Harvard classmate in the early 1900s, "and I am going to put a lot more into it than I'll ever be paid for." With a proven record on East River subway tunnels, the young Holland in 1919 was appointed chief engineer of an automobile tunnel beneath the Hudson River that would connect Manhattan and New Jersey. Holland's obsession with the project subsequently ruined his health. He died at age 41 in 1924, never to see his tunnel completed. It opened on November 12, 1927, slightly more than seven years after excavation had begun.

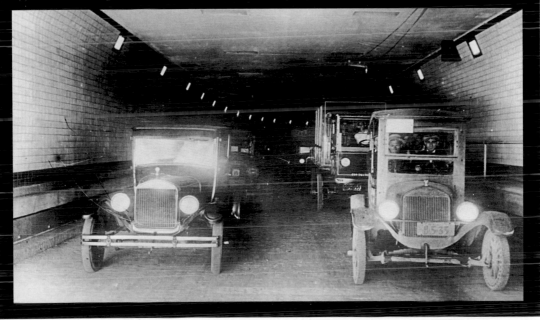

THE CHANNEL TUNNEL: "There are few projects against which there exists a deeper and more enduring prejudice than the construction of a railway tunnel between Dover and Calais," said Winston Churchill in 1936.

Indeed, it has taken two and a half centuries to realize the dream of a trans-Channel link between Great Britain and France. Contractors even started to dig twice, in the early 1880s and again in 1974.

Finally, in 1987, excavation began on the Channel Tunnel, a project financed, built, and operated by Eurotunnel, an Anglo-French company. Transmanche Link, an Anglo-French joint venture, contracted for the construction work. On December 1, 1990, crews of both countries shook hands some 200 feet below the seabed in the tunnel breakthrough, uniting the two shores in a fixed link.

The 31-mile-long, three-tunnel "Chunnel," as the British call it, boasts the world's longest underwater section at 24 miles and is the world's second longest rail tunnel, containing four different train systems.

Above: **Inside the Chunnel a tunnel boring machine (TBM) dwarfs a construction worker *(right)* standing before its rotary drilling head. Chalk marl from the excavation cakes the leviathan's tungsten cutting head.**

Left: **A worker inspects reinforced concrete tunnel-lining segments en route to the tunnel boring machine in the French undersea north rail tunnel at Calais.**

With building costs topping 21 billion dollars, the tunnel is also history's most expensive privately financed tunnel engineering project.

Construction of the tunnel involved both ancient and state-of-the-art engineering. Surveyors aligned facing tunnel sections using navigation satellites, triangulation, and plumb lines. Guided by both computer-linked lasers and dead reckoning, technicians some 200 feet below the seabed advanced massive tunnel boring machines, or TBMs—the cutting edge of tunneling.

Traveling from both directions, the TBMs simultaneously lined the tunnels with concrete or cast-iron segments. Ejected chalk marl was transported to the surface for disposal. Near midpoint, the British TBMs nosedived into the Channel floor for permanent burial, enabling the French to complete the breakthrough.

Completed in 1994, the project posed huge logistical and technical challenges, such as how to transport workers, supplies, and equipment to the headings and how to remove millions of tons of spoil. The builders had to maneuver huge machines through wet and muck, debug new technologies, and fix jammed conveyors. Despite setbacks, delays, and soaring costs, the Channel Tunnel has earned its place as a landmark of 20th-century civil engineering. ■

The shuttle train, a rail ferry service, travels inside the Channel Tunnel, en route to France.

Opposite: Walter P. Chrysler wanted a building "that would not merely scrape the sky but positively pierce it." The Chrysler Building was briefly the world's tallest.

Skyscrapers

NO OTHER TOTEMS TO THE MODERN AGE are more compelling than the gravity-defying, vertical shafts of glass, steel, and concrete known as skyscrapers. In little more than a century, skyscrapers have proliferated throughout the world, now dominating the skyline of nearly every major city.

While ubiquitous today, the skyscraper is a native American architectural form. Its emergence in Chicago in the late 1800s was due to several factors: a booming economy, the increased value of urban space, and the work of a few brilliant engineers. The devastating fire of 1871 also played a role, giving businessmen the chance to rebuild much of downtown Chicago. Architect William Le Baron Jenney's Leiter

THE LANDMARK HOME INSURANCE BUILDING, completed in Chicago in 1885, was designed by William Le Baron Jenney (1832-1907), a local civil engineer known today as the father of the skyscraper. The iron-and-steel-framed building contained many features common to later skyscrapers.

Building, with its open facade of steel and glass, triggered the evolution in 1879. His Home Insurance Building followed. Though it broke no height records, the ten-story building contained features found on later skyscrapers. Its upper stories were built with Bessemer steel instead of cast iron, and it relied on a steel-and-iron frame, not a masonry wall, to support much of its weight.

Modern skyscraper technology originated in the 19th century. The invention of the I-beam was especially important. The beam derived its name from a thin vertical plate that linked horizontal flanges along the top and bottom length of the beam. Greater vertical depth gave the beam more stiffness with only a modest amount of added steel. Mass production of such beams in many standard sizes made the construction of tall buildings economical and allowed their performance to be calculated more exactly. Reinforced concrete also provided a new and economical method of carrying large loads, and engineers learned how to calculate the behavior of the new material.

The appearance of the elevator was another crucial development. Until Elisha Otis's invention in the 1850s, buildings were limited to heights people could walk up comfortably—usually just a few stories.

That a strong, internal steel skeleton could now support great weight while remaining light—and that it had reliable tensile strength and a much higher compression strength—encouraged the design of buildings that could soar beyond the limits of traditional masonry structures. Without the need for heavy exterior walls, engineers could now drape the frame with non-load-bearing materials. Not only did buildings look different—with glass-and-steel shells, marble facades, and fireproof materials—but their occupants benefited from light, air, and safety. ■

BUILDING THE EMPIRE STATE: For most people, the history of skyscrapers begins in earnest with the Empire State Building, whose 1,250-foot height and graduated shape help define New York's skyline. Completed well ahead of schedule in 1931, it remained the world's tallest building for four decades, eclipsed only by the 1973 World Trade Center and then by Chicago's 1974 Sears Tower.

Built during the Depression, the building was the center of a competition between Walter Chrysler, founder of the Chrysler Corporation, and John Jakob Raskob, a former executive of General Motors, to see who could construct the tallest building.

Architect William Lamb, admirer of the perpendicular designs of Eliel Saarinen, chose as his design concept the simple pencil; the pencil's clean, soaring lines inspired him. The Empire State Building rose amazingly fast: Its 85 stories were finished within 18 months. The gradually recessed walls, or setbacks, were required by New York City's cautious building codes. In 1945, dramatic proof of the skyscraper's stability came when a U.S. Air Force B-25 crashed into the 72nd and 73rd floors, causing damage but no real danger to the overall structure.

The stiff internal skeleton contains 57,000 tons of steel beams, connected by rivets and bolts and strengthened with portal bracing. Beams, posts, windows, and window frames, made in factories and moved to the site by a small-gauge railway, were transported skyward by derricks and electric hoists. As many as 38 five-man riveting teams performed the

Its mast originally designed for anchoring zeppelins, the 1,250-foot Empire State Building remains the world's ninth tallest building at press time.

Right: **A blue-collar acrobat secures a cable one-quarter of a mile above the streets of New York.**

Bottom: **At a lower level, members of the hoisting gang attach cables to bundles of girders and then give the high sign, sending the steel skyward.**

difficult and precarious job of sinking red-hot rivets into predrilled holes in the steel. As the rivets cooled, they shrank, solidly fixing the connections.

Daily timetables and progress reports tracked, numbered, and designated steel beams, bricks, window frames, and other building materials. Construction ran with such precision that many steel beams were riveted into place only three days after leaving the Pittsburgh steel mills, some 300 miles away. ◼

A SKYSCRAPER TIMELINE: The modern period of skyscrapers began after the steel frames and diagonal bracing necessary to resist wind pressure were refined during the 1920s and 1930s, preparing the way for post–World War II skyscrapers. In the 1950s and 1960s, many buildings were entirely sheathed in non-load-bearing materials like glass, a technique known as curtain-wall construction. Inexpensive energy for air conditioning was an important prerequisite for these "glass boxes," inspired by the work of Ludwig Mies van der Rohe, whose International Style in skyscraper building set the style for the next two decades.

Beginning in the early 1960s, many of the most exciting skyscrapers featured tubular design, in which the walls were treated as a rigid tube, allowing much of the internal bracing to be removed and affording a great amount of internal room. Walls once again bore loads but now could be both light *and* strong. With much of the gravity load and nearly all of the wind load carried by the exterior walls, engineers and architects began to explore new forms to express structure in skyscrapers.

With concrete, this led to buildings that display the smooth transfer of forces from closely spaced wall columns above to large, widely spaced columns at street level, as, for example, in Houston's Two Shell Plaza.

In steel, it led to an exterior X-braced tower for Chicago's John Hancock Center, finished in 1968, which required much less steel than traditional designs, while maintaining stiffness against wind loads. The bundled tube design of the Sears Tower, completed in 1974, also in Chicago, was a technological breakthrough in which nine bundled tubes, each 75 feet square, are interlocked, each serving to reinforce the others. At regular intervals the tubes stop, leaving only two that rise to the 110th floor.

At 1,454 feet, the Sears Tower remained the world's tallest for a quarter century, until the height record was claimed by the Petronas Towers in Malaysia. The Taipei 101 Tower seized the height record in 2004, only to be outdone by Dubai's Burj Tower, which was still under construction at press time.

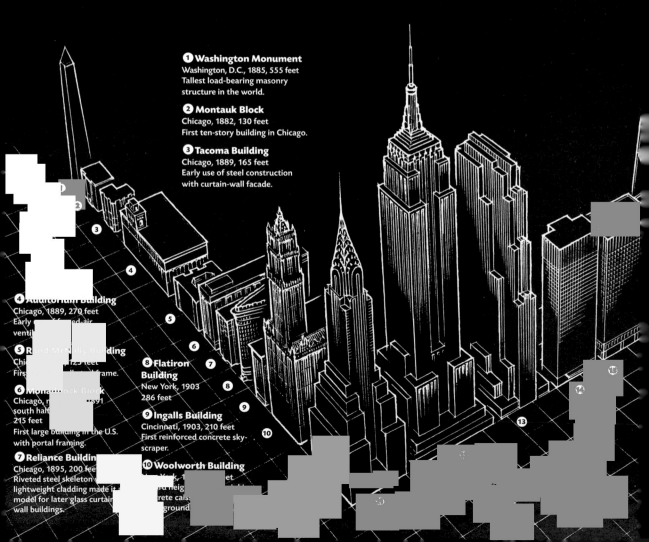

❶ Washington Monument
Washington, D.C., 1885, 555 feet
Tallest load-bearing masonry structure in the world.

❷ Montauk Block
Chicago, 1882, 130 feet
First ten-story building in Chicago.

❸ Tacoma Building
Chicago, 1889, 165 feet
Early use of steel construction with curtain-wall facade.

❹ Auditorium Building
Chicago, 1889, 270 feet
Early use of forced-air ventil

❺ Rand McNally Building
Chi   125 feet
Firs   frame.

❻ Monadnock Block
Chicago,   1891
south half
215 feet
First large building in the U.S. with portal framing.

❼ Reliance Building
Chicago, 1895, 200 feet
Riveted steel skeleton
lightweight cladding made it
model for later glass curtain
wall buildings.

❽ Flatiron Building
New York, 1903
286 feet

❾ Ingalls Building
Cincinnati, 1903, 210 feet
First reinforced concrete skyscraper.

❿ Woolworth Building
    York,   et
        and heig
         rete cais
         ground

Right: With a giant 60-foot spire inspired by Taiwan's native bamboo plant, the Taipei 101 Tower stands pagoda-like in downtown Taipei. Completed in December 2004, the tower rises 1,667 feet. It was eclipsed in August 2007 by the Burj Tower in Dubai, United Arab Emirates, which when finished in 2008 will be the world's tallest.

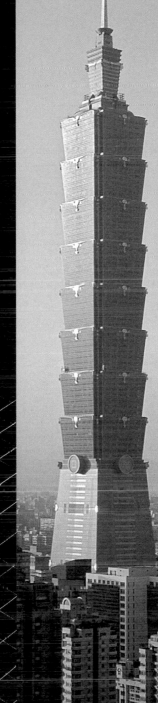

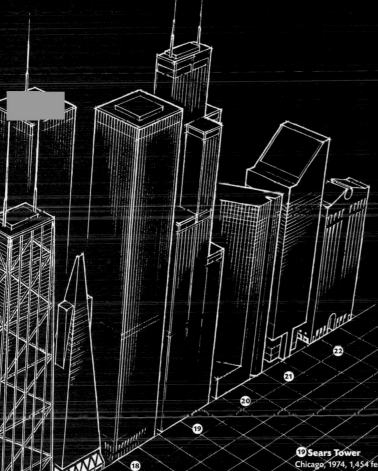

11 Chrysler Building
New York, 1930, 1,046 feet

12 Empire State Building
New York, 1931, 1,250 feet
Third tallest building in the world today.

13 RCA Building
New York, 1933, 850 feet
Part of first large-scale skyscraper complex.

14 Seagram Building
New York, 1958, 525 feet
Prototype of the glass-and-metal, flat-topped high rise.

15 Brunswick Building
Chicago, 1965, 475 feet
Load-bearing concrete walls freed interior space of columns.

16 John Hancock Center
Chicago, 1968, 1,127 feet
Exterior steel diagonals brace against wind shear.

17 Transamerica Building
San Francisco, 1972, 853 feet
Foundation designed to resist earthquakes.

18 World Trade Center
New York, 1973
1,368 feet
1,362 feet
Second tallest building in the world; metal-mesh skin supported large share of building's weight.

19 Sears Tower
Chicago, 1974, 1,454 feet
World's tallest building; bundled tubes resist wind.

20 John Hancock Tower
Boston, 1976, 790 feet

21 Citicorp Center
New York, 1977, 919 feet
Computerized dampers on roof counteract movement caused by wind.

22 AT&T Headquarters
New York, 1984, 647 feet
Granite curtain wall simulates heavy masonry.

HONG KONG: The skyline and city lights of Hong Kong, looking toward Victoria Harbor and Kowloon, are seen by night from Victoria Peak.

A former British colony returned to China in 1997, Hong Kong (the name means "fragrant harbor") is a major seaport, financial center, and dominant business hub of Asia. A city of opportunities, extremes, and energetic street life, the tiny portion of flat land available for construction (estimated to be less than 80 square miles) has led to a concentrated high-rise environment and extremely high population density.

During the 1980s Hong Kong engineers added high technology to its crowded cement-and-glass-box skyline with such skyscrapers as the Hongkong and Shanghai Bank headquarters building and the Bank of China, symbols of the city's aspirations for the future.

HONG KONG BANKS: Few cities have the concentration of skyscrapers—or banks—of Hong Kong. Two rivals, finished in the late 1980s and located two blocks apart, have drawn special attention: one, the Hongkong and Shanghai Banking Corporation, for its dramatic, high-tech appearance; the other, the Bank of China, for its highly innovative structure.

Below: Built by architect Norman Foster and the firm of Ove Arup & Partners, the Hongkong Bank's floors hang from five massive, aluminum-clad suspension trusses.

In the Hongkong Bank, eight masts, lined up along the perimeter of the building, absorb its weight, resulting in an open floor plan. At five points, large suspension trusses form two-story triangles, which carry the loads of the floors to the masts.

Much more economical, the 70-story Bank of China was to many the finest skyscraper since Ludwig Mies van der Rohe's Seagram Building of 1958. Architect I. M. Pei and engineer Leslie Robertson relied on a "megastructure"—a triangular trussed grid of glass and metal—instead of the usual steel frame. No internal diagonal wind bracing was needed, and the design called for 40 percent less steel than usual in buildings of similar height. ■

Top: Computerized, mirrorlike "sunscoops" fill the Hongkong Bank's atrium with sunlight.

Opposite: Showpiece of the Beijing government in Hong Kong, the 1,209-foot, glass-and-aluminum-clad Bank of China dominates the cityscape.

3: PUBLIC SPACES

Sports Arenas
Exposition Halls

OVER THE AGES, GREAT INGENUITY has been devoted to creating functional buildings for large-scale public entertainments. As many as 55,000 spectators in ancient Rome's huge Colosseum cheered gladiators from beneath a retractable awning whose supports, anchored in the exterior walls, afforded unimpeded views. Today, 150,000 soccer fans applaud their teams from seating in Rio de Janeiro's Maracanã Stadium, with its reinforced concrete roof.

Development of roofs for immense arenas required major technological advances. New materials were sought to construct roofs able to bridge huge inner spaces and strong enough to withstand the resulting stress. Since concrete had been stretched to its limits, 19th-century engineers experimented with lighter structures made of iron, steel, or concrete reinforced with steel.

Public exhibition space was suddenly in demand. Proud of their industrial progress, nations gathered in London to display their products at the first world's fair in 1851. The star attraction was the exposition hall itself, the Crystal Palace. A shimmering vision of sheet-glass panels supported by a cast-iron-and-wood framework, it heralded a new era of large buildings assembled out of mostly mass-produced parts. A singular virtue lay in ease of construction.

Buildings with glass vaulted roofs or curtain walls—from 19th-century retail arcades such as Moscow's Trade Halls (known also as the GUM department store) to Canada's West Edmonton Mall and Paris's Pompidou Center—are functional descendants of the Crystal Palace. Here visitors can stroll in spacious surroundings, undisturbed by weather or traffic. Both exposition halls and sports arenas need a maximum amount of open space to set off displays and accommodate throngs of visitors. In an arena spectators need unobstructed views of the playing field. As a result, most arenas and exposition halls lack interior load-bearing walls, thus placing additional stress on exterior walls and roofs.

Engineers have learned to manage this stress. Interior or exterior steel frameworks support lightweight panels of glass, steel, or plastic, producing some wondrously airy-looking structures, such as the Pontiac Silverdome in Michigan and the Hoosier Dome in Indianapolis, which span several acres. One day, such technology may be adapted to improve conditions for those in the world's harsher climates. ■

Preceding pages: **Against the backdrop of a newer Rome, the ruins of the Temples of Saturn and Vespasian rise from the ancient Roman Forum.**

Left: **The colorful pipes of the Georges Pompidou National Art and Culture Center in Paris were designed by architects Richard Rogers and Renzo Piano.**

Opposite: **The Colosseum owes its permanence to a design as rock solid as its 40-foot-deep foundation.**

Sports Arenas

AMONG THE LARGEST AND MOST IMPOSING of all public places are those built for sports; today, as in ancient Greece and Rome, most sizable cities boast at least one stadium or arena.

In the fourth century B.C. the Greeks erected a stadium at Olympia, site of the original Olympic Games. Primitive in design, the stadium took advantage of the topography. One side of the field nestles against a hill; heaped earth around the other sides forms huge, sloping embankments for spectators. Other Greek builders refined this design, cutting terraces into hillsides and lining them with stone seats. In Roman hands the Greek stadium became the freestanding stone amphitheater, the largest of which

Finished in 1975, the Louisiana Superdome boasts a system of movable grandstands that give it great versatility.

was the Colosseum. These amphitheaters fell to ruin with the Roman Empire. Not until the late 1800s, with renewed interest in large-scale spectator sports, would such huge arenas again be built.

In the 20th century the evolution of football, ice hockey, and other sports led to stadiums tailored to particular needs, although in recent decades the trend has shifted again toward more versatile designs. Houston's 1965 steel-roofed Astrodome, with a seating capacity of 74,000, was among the first of these multiuse, roofed stadiums. It was succeeded by Seattle's Kingdome in reinforced and prestressed concrete and then by the Louisiana Superdome in steel. Fabric-roofed structures have also appeared. Air pressure holds up some, such as the Silverdome in Pontiac, Michigan; others, like the Munich Olympic Stadium, assume a tentlike form. ∎

THE COLOSSEUM: As enduring as the Eternal City itself, the Colosseum stands as a haunting reminder of Roman grandeur. Even so, two-thirds of the original structure has vanished, lost to the elements, vandals, souvenir hunters, and medieval construction crews who used the building as a quarry.

What remains owes its permanence to a rock-solid design. Construction took ten years and began in A.D. 70 on orders from the emperor Vespasian. He envisioned nothing less than the largest structure of its kind—615 feet long, 510 feet wide, 159 feet high, and more than a third of a mile in circumference. Ground was not so much broken as drained, since the emperor had chosen an artificial lake as the site. Concrete soon

An aerial view of the Colosseum shows its striking similarity to many modern stadiums and arenas. Concentric tiers of seats could hold as many as 55,000 spectators.

Above: Inside, the Colosseum was a honeycomb of vaulted corridors and stairways made of brick-faced concrete.

Below: **The basement shows Roman engineering skill. From here, caged animals were hoisted to the upper level. Once the cages were opened, the beasts could escape— but only up a ramp and through a trapdoor into the arena** *(red arrows).* **Nets on top of the wall surrounding the arena provided protection from rampaging animals.**

replaced water, and powerful travertine piers, set on the concrete foundation, were linked radially by arches, walls, and vaults—mostly of brick-faced concrete—to make five concentric rings. On this structure more arches, walls, and vaults were erected to support three levels of sloping stone seats.

Up to 55,000 spectators could fit into the stadium for a full day's entertainment in the central arena. A parade of chariots might open the spectacle, which would include gladiatorial games and wild beast hunts. Boxers, horsemen, and archers might perform, but it was the blood sports that drew cheers. For most events, the arena was spread with sand to absorb spilled blood, although on occasion it was flooded with water to set the stage for a mock naval battle. ■

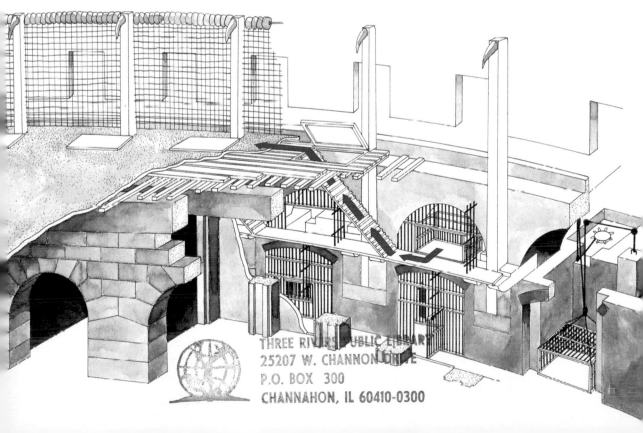

Workers unroll artificial turf, nicknamed Mardi Grass, before a baseball game. Movable seats on the lower level have been fully retracted to make full use of the space.

THE LOUISIANA SUPERDOME: Rising 27 stories above the New Orleans streets and covering 10 acres, the Louisiana Superdome is the largest of all enclosed stadiums. A system of movable grandstands gives the Superdome its versatility, allowing it to expand from a relatively compact arena seating as few as 20,000 spectators, to a football stadium with room for 84,000, to a convention or concert hall holding more than 100,000.

The building posed immense challenges: The steel dome was the largest ever attempted, and the sheer weight of the edifice, with its 169,000 cubic yards of concrete and 20,000 tons of steel, would generate massive compression. To cope with the compressive forces, the design called for some 2,100 prestressed concrete pilings to be driven 165 feet into bedrock. Five thousand additional pilings would form the underpinning for the stadium's underground garage and for the concrete slab beneath the playing field.

As for the dome, a skeleton of steel ribs provided its backbone. These radial ribs were linked by a series of concentric struts and further strengthened by cross-bracing to create a framework of hundreds of small lattice trusses. To facilitate the roof's construction, builders set up temporary supports. Once complete, the roof was jacked down as a single unit onto its permanent support—a huge steel tension ring 680 feet in diameter. The tension ring is a significant structural component; without it, the dome would collapse. A circular truss made of 1½-inch-thick steel, the ring

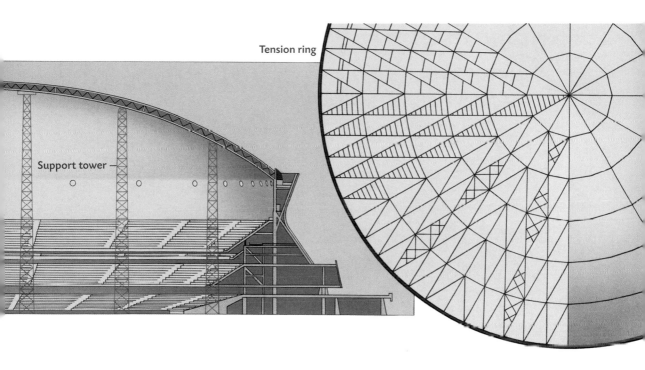

Tension ring

Support tower

was prefabricated in 24 sections, each lifted into position, 169 feet up, before being welded to adjoining sections. The welding took place in a tent-house that was moved from joint to joint as work progressed. Finally, each weld was x-rayed to ensure its integrity.

The roof was designed with an unjointed skin that would "breathe," rising and falling as much as three inches in response to fluctuations in temperature and wind pressure. In addition, the pinned connections linking the vertical columns to the tension ring allowed up to eight inches of movement.

Residents of New Orleans were forced to take refuge in the Superdome when Hurricane Katrina struck the city in the summer of 2005. The loss of electric power and water caused several days of suffering for those inside the arena, but the structure held through the storm itself. The winds tore away two small sections of the roof that were repaired the following year. ■

Top: A diagram of the roof's framework shows the tension ring and the lattice trusses created by intersecting radiating ribs, concentric struts, and cross-braces. In the cross section, the roof's temporary support towers are visible.

Below: These examples of different seating configurations reflect the Superdome's great versatility.

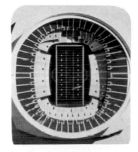

Football

Baseball

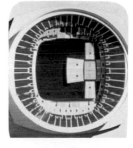
Arena

Convention

Opposite: **Completed in 1982, Epcot Center's Spaceship Earth was on the cutting edge of design and technology.**

Exposition Halls

FEW PUBLIC PLACES HAVE A GREATER NEED to enclose more space with the least amount of material than those built to house expositions. Large exposition halls are a relatively modern phenomenon, the product of lighter and stronger building materials that can span great spaces without collapsing. In fact, it wasn't until 1851, with the building of the Crystal Palace at the first world's fair in London, that the exposition hall truly came of age, and with it came the modern era of prefabricated, modular construction.

Over the ensuing decades, "crystal-palace construction" became the inspiration for other temporary exposition halls, as well as for permanent arcades, galleries, and other new building types worldwide.

Later in the 19th century, the introduction of space-frame construction, in which stresses are equally distributed within a three-dimensional structure composed of interconnected members, marked yet another advance in the evolution of the exposition hall. The form achieved a kind of perfection in 1982 with Epcot Center's Spaceship Earth in Florida, the first monumental geodesic sphere.

First patented in 1954 by R. Buckminster Fuller, an American architect and engineer, geodesic domes have become popular as an inexpensive and environmentally efficient way to enclose space. ■

Below: **The Crystal Palace, London, 1851**

Encased in nearly one million square feet of glass, the Crystal Palace heralded today's glass-curtain buildings.

THE CRYSTAL PALACE: It was the Great Exhibition of the Works of Industry of All Nations, the first world's fair, and when it opened in 1851 more than eight miles of tables displayed such wonders as false teeth, artificial legs, and chewing tobacco.

But for many of the six million visitors to London's Great Exhibition, the most intriguing object displayed was not inside the building but the building itself, the "Crystal Palace," as it became known. This stunning work had been conceived not by an architect but by a horticulturist named Joseph Paxton, a farmer's son with little formal education. Its design had taken just eight days and the construction of its entire frame a mere 17 weeks.

Considered one of history's most influential buildings for the technology it introduced, the Crystal Palace looked like an overgrown greenhouse, its long, stepped, rectangular main hall bisected by a high, vaulted transept and topped by a pleated, ridge-and-furrow roof. Hollow iron columns doubled as downspouts, removing rainwater collected in the fluted rafters forming the furrows of the roof. Diagonal wrought-iron rods, crossed to form X-shaped portal braces, linked each horizontal beam to pairs of vertical columns. Together with the roof's trussed girders, these portal braces gave the exterior walls the rigidity required to compensate for the absence of interior walls. In all, the hall held some 4,500 tons of cast and wrought iron, 600,000

Iron columns and glass-sheathed roof trusses created a vast interior space awash in daylight. The transept, reaching almost 110 feet high, easily accommodated a fountain and several live elm trees.

cubic feet of wood (used in the gutters, mullions, and interior arches), and 900,000 square feet of sheet glass; it covered 19 acres of London's Hyde Park. Yet despite its size, the hall had a modular design and prefabricated components that allowed it to come down as easily as it had gone up. In fact, the design incorporated just two different story heights, three different widths, and seven different iron components. Hence, many of the components could be cast in standard lengths at foundries elsewhere in England, brought by rail to London, and assembled on-site. ■

DESIGNED TO CELEBRATE FRENCH INDUSTRIAL PROWESS, the 1889 Paris Exhibition also marked the centenary of the French Revolution. The Gallery of Machines, on the Champs de Mars opposite the Eiffel Tower, was itself an engineering triumph. Framed in steel—the new stronger material—instead of iron like the Crystal Palace, the Gallery's glass panels were fixed to its exterior, shaping a vast inner space. Pairs of hinged girders formed arches spanning 380 feet and soaring to 140 feet. The pin supports at the arches' tops and beneath their bearing-plates allowed the building to flex if its metal expanded or contracted or if the ground supports shifted.

WEST EDMONTON MALL: Under construction from 1981 to 1998, the West Edmonton Mall boasts the world's largest shopping center and parking lot and was built in four phases. Phase three in 1985 included the world's largest indoor wave pool.

Spanning the equivalent of 104 football fields, the structure of the mall is steel throughout, with a clear-span glazed 400-by-100-foot dome, carried on two-foot-deep steel-plated curved roof beams. The mall is the first development in Canada that added large-scale entertainment to the retail experience. Ranging from electronics playgrounds to stores designed as movie sets, these new outlets sell fantasy as well as tangible goods.

GALLERIA VITTORIO: Joseph Paxton's glass palace inspired dreams of more elaborate creations. He imagined a "Great Victorian Way," a glass-enclosed compound to encircle London. Such ideas brought new life to a form that both grew up and died out in the 1800s: the arcade. The first vaulted glass-roof arcade was built about 1830 for Paris's Galerie d'Orléans.

Arcades evolved from a need for protected public spaces that could handle crowd flow; glass had the advantage of providing light, transparency, and shelter. Arcades served a number of social purposes—department stores, markets—often becoming hubs of public life. They also served as models for other building types, such as a means of access in prisons, the railroad station, and the bath house.

One of the most influential arcades was Milan's monumental Galleria Vittorio Emanuele II. Dedicated in 1867, it served as a covered promenade between the city's cathedral and opera house. Its massive dome, supported by arch beams, rises some 130 feet. Circumferential supports hold ribbing that secures overlapping panes of glass, through which light showers on a quarter-acre rotunda.

During the 1800s, glass-enclosed arcades expanded in size. The largest was Moscow's 1893 Trade Halls, an 820-foot-long glass barrel vault with a very light roof and multileveled access to more than 1,000 interior units. For the first time, an arcade was its own spatial system, not a connection to something. It pointed the way to the American shopping center, a 1950s creation grown immense in Minnesota's 4.2-million-square-foot Mall of America, opened in 1992. ■

The glass umbrella of Milan's magnificent Galleria Vittorio Emanuele II remains, as it has for more than a century, *il cuore della città*—**"the heart of the city."**

4: THE NEED FOR

PROTECTION

On Land
From Water

PEOPLE HAVE BUILT BARRIERS since Neolithic times. As early as 8000 B.C., the city of Jericho was protected by a wall 13 feet high and 10 feet thick. Military strategy in classical Greece often called for walls and counter-walls. In China, the Great Wall stands today as a testament to the tenacity of its builders. In some civilizations, barriers not only enclosed a city but defined it as well.

Walled strongholds served both as defenses and as symbols of power. Openings in a wall were guarded as carefully as spillways in an irrigation system. Fortified gates discouraged attacking armies and encouraged respect. Walls endure as prominent features of cities such as York, Carcassonne, and Istanbul.

In 11th-century England, castles and their defending walls were simply high mounds topped with wooden towers, surrounded by a ditch with a series of barricades. Changes in castle construction came slowly, often following weaponry advances. Wooden barricades gave way to stone walls. Towers with square corners that could easily be taken by siege equipment assumed new shapes. Emphasis shifted away from tower defenses to virtually impregnable walls.

By the 14th century, the concentric castle—a circuit of walls and towers surrounded by another, lower circuit of battered walls with towers of its own—proved highly successful against invaders. Only powerful siege guns, developed in the late 14th century, could force castle occupants into submission.

Humans have always sought proximity to water, crucial to both agriculture and trade, but the downside is flood risk. Some flooding can be beneficial; for example, the fertile silt laid down each year by the Nile supported the ancient Egyptians' agriculture. Just as often, though, flooding brings devastation: Inundations caused by seasonal melts, severe storms, and flood tides have killed thousands worldwide and wreaked havoc on land along coasts and riverbanks.

Ancient anti-flood measures include earthen levees, dams, and dikes. Modern flood control uses many of the same techniques but on a larger scale and with new technological complexity. But even state-of-the-art projects such as the Dutch Deltaplan and the Thames Barrier may one day answer to the all-powerful sea. ■

Preceding pages: **Nestled against the snowcapped peaks of the Sierra Nevada in southern Spain, the Alhambra commands a 35-acre plateau above Granada, recalling an era of foreign conquest. No invader ever stormed the Alhambra's walls.**

Left: **The Thames Barrier spans the river eight miles downstream from London. Movable gates rise 60 feet against surge tides; during this early exercise, one gate remains open to shipping.**

On Land

ARCHAEOLOGY TELLS US THAT EARLY CIVILIZATIONS commonly built walls. Made of wood or mud brick and later of stone or fired brick, defensive barriers grew higher. They protected homesteads, towns, and even entire city-states.

Well into medieval times, walls were the key to defense against enemies on land, whether marauding neighbors or invading foreign armies.

Fortress construction changed over time. Earlier square or rectangular construction employed thick, high walls and few openings. Thick walls were effective walls. Engineers added bulk economically by building shells of stone or masonry and filling them with rubble. Walls within walls were even better; if the enemy broke through the outer defense, the defenders could rally from the inner enclosure.

Special attention was given to the keep, used as both residence and refuge. Gradually, dependence on rectangular stone keeps—for passive defense—yielded to emphasis on circular towers of lighter construction. These allowed a wider field of vision and thus a more active defense.

Gunpowder and other advances eventually rendered immense walled fortifications obsolete. But walls would take on a new purpose in military forts designed to give superior advantage to the placement of cannon. ■

CUTAWAY VIEW OF DOVER CASTLE KEEP

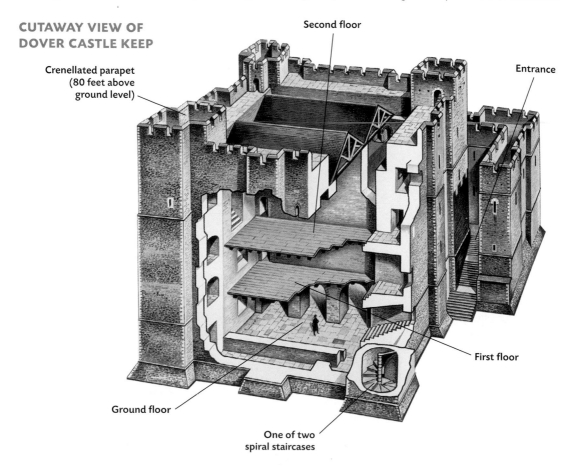

Second floor

Crenellated parapet (80 feet above ground level)

Entrance

First floor

Ground floor

One of two spiral staircases

Spotlights illuminate Caernarvon's crenellated walls and polygonal towers. The castle epitomizes the fortress building style during the age of Edward I of England.

CAERNARVON CASTLE: To subdue Welsh resistance, Edward I of England spent much of his reign building fortresses to establish his presence in Wales. Many stood along the northwest coast, where they could be supplied and reinforced from the sea.

Grandest of all, Caernarvon commands a site at the mouth of the River Seiont, overlooking the Menai Strait. From its beginnings in 1283, Edward envisioned Caernarvon as a vice-regal center and the seat of the Prince of Wales; in fact, he bestowed the title on a son born there in 1284.

Caernarvon was built on a site containing the ruins of a Roman fort and Norman castle. Its concentric plan measured roughly 570 by 200 feet, with an inner wall and an irregularly angled outer wall. On the exposed southern side, the outer wall was thicker and higher, supporting three tiers of stations for defending archers. Thirteen polygonal towers protected the outer wall. Though symmetrically placed, no two towers are alike.

Two towers formed the castle's main focus: An immense gatehouse, facing north into the walled town, opened into a 60-foot passage plugged with six

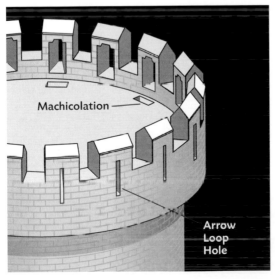

Machicolation

Arrow
Loop
Hole

retractable iron gates and five sets of double doors. All this was protected from above by numerous arrow loops and seven sets of machicolations (overhanging defensive structures for discharging arrows). Instead of a central keep, the Eagle Tower rose 124 feet along the western wall. It could be shut off and supplied from outside through its own water gate.

Aspects of Caernarvon's design, such as the polygonal towers and bands of colored stonework, can be traced to the walls of Constantinople. ■

At a distance, medieval castles present immense, forbidding facades to the outside world. Close up, they reveal many innovations, such as round towers and arrow loop holes, that gave advantage to the defenders.

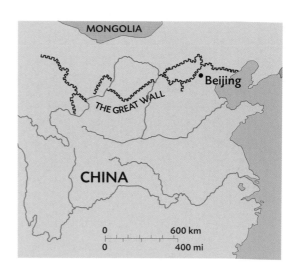

THE GREAT WALL: Regarded as one of the most ambitious engineering projects ever, the Great Wall of China was built by hundreds of thousands of laborers over several centuries—at an unknown cost in lives. Now partially restored, the wall extends from the desert in Gansu Province to the sea at Shanhaiguan on the east coast. It takes advantage of

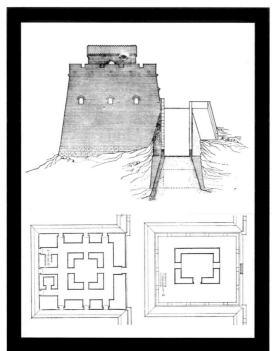

THROUGHOUT its lengthy course, the Great Wall incorporated a variety of defensive structures, many of which had proved effective in city walls. Building materials varied with the resources available at different locations. The drawing above shows a guardhouse erected near a gate in remote Shanxi Province during the Ming dynasty, when almost all of the wall existing today was built. A ramp on the inner side of the wall leads to the two-level structure (*diagrams*), which housed a small garrison. Capable of supporting cannon, the guardhouse, along with a nearby observation tower and signal tower, formed a defense and communications unit, one of many unifying security along the wall's entire length.

the defensive features of the land, often by following a ridge and then doubling back on itself to command the high ground.

Qin Shihuang, the First Emperor, began building border defenses in the third century B.C. to protect his newly unified domain from invaders. He commandeered a huge workforce of both civilians and soldiers. Sections of earlier walls were linked with new construction. Almost no evidence of the Qin wall remains to reveal its location or details of its structure.

Today's wall arose gradually, in response to repeated northern threats. The wall was punctuated by some 25,000 watchtowers, gates, castles, guardhouses, and even temples and shrines. Beacon towers every 11 miles signaled other outposts of attack, and paths on the wall's crest permitted movement of troops.

Though a formidable barrier, the Great Wall failed to stop northern nomadic peoples or the Manchu invaders who became China's rulers after they entered Beijing in 1644. Although the wall was neglected for long periods, sections have been rebuilt and restoration continues today. ∎

Top: Built and rebuilt over several centuries, the Great Wall winds some 2,000 miles through northern China to the Yellow Sea.

Opposite: The wall takes a tortuous path along ridges in the mountains northeast of Beijing.

SACSAHUAMAN: The jagged, terraced walls of Sacsahuaman, a 15th-century Inca stronghold, zigzag along a steep rise above Cuzco, in Peru. Sacsahuaman's stonework is remarkable for any era. It is not known how the large stone blocks were hauled to the building site, often over many miles without wheeled transport. With only stone hammers and bronze crowbars, masons dressed and custom-fitted each stone in place, creating tight, mortarless joints. Masons shaped the face of each stone into a rounded bulge, tapering at the edges, and meticulously fit them together like pieces of a jigsaw puzzle. Inca builders took no shortcuts in their work. Up to 60 feet high, the walls still have joints so tight that a knife blade cannot fit between them. So heavy yet flexible were the walls that they have survived earthquakes.

From Water

THE OPTION OFFERED TO NOAH as a defense against flooding was unique. Most inhabitants of flood-prone areas—now estimated at one-tenth of the world's population—have found it necessary to develop other means of protection against overflowing rivers and encroaching seas.

Over the millennia, flood-control engineers have pursued two basic strategies: building barriers such as dikes and levees or lowering the water level. The latter approach requires the storage of water in swamps or mountain reservoirs for either controlled or gradual natural release.

These strategies hold worldwide, though the technologies used may vary. Both Bangladesh and the Netherlands, for example, are low-lying countries imperiled by the sea. With few resources except manpower, Bangladesh relies chiefly on traditional technology. The Netherlands, on the other hand, has drawn on centuries of flood-control experience and the latest advances in hydraulic engineering, and foresight has allowed engineers to respond quickly to disaster.

Since flooding is a natural phenomenon that cannot be prevented, long-term solutions must also take into account best management practices in agriculture, urban planning, and water resources management. ∎

Rows of clay-filled bags create a makeshift barrier against the sea in Bangladesh.

Above: An engineering project begun 2,000 years ago in China still diverts the Min River in Sichuan Province. A man-made island divides the Min into two channels.

THE GUAN XIAN FLOOD PROJECT:

Every spring, according to a 19th-century account, people in the western Chinese province of Sichuan would attend a ceremony dating back more than 2,000 years. Before dawn, a visiting dignitary would burn incense and offer prayers to the gods and to the memory of two third-century B.C. officials, Li Bing and his son, Li Erlang. Then he would leave the temple erected for the worship of Li Erlang and proceed to the bank of the Min River. There, the people would watch as a band of laborers pulled a bamboo cable to breach a temporary cofferdam, unleashing the waters of the Min for irrigation.

The diversion of the Min River forms the basis of the Guan Xian flood control project, begun about

250 B.C. The Min runs low in winter but is subject to heavy flooding during spring thaws and summer rains. Controlling it meant an end to droughts and floods, and transformed this area of China into one of its most productive.

The visionary behind the project, Li Bing, was administrator of the ancient province of Shu. His plan divided the Min into an inner channel for irrigation and an outer one to carry normal flow and runoff, as well as river traffic to the Yangtze. Li Bing accomplished this using hand labor and local materials of wood and stone. His workers began by piling stones in the middle of the Min's natural channel, building a long embankment, or division-head, to divide it.

Bottom: **The illustration shows the channel division and the canal called Neck of the Precious Bottle, which cuts through a mountain to irrigate more than 1,400 square miles of farmland today. The spillway sends surplus water to the outer channel and on downriver.**

To direct the inner channel onto the Chengdu Plain, they cut a 90-foot-wide canal through a nearby mountain. The water that was thus diverted eastward was channeled through a system of feeder canals, conduits, spillways, and lesser conduits to supply 2,000 square miles of farmland, serving a population of five million. Through a spillway, the excess water was rerouted to the outer channel and on downriver.

After Li Bing died, the project was finished by his son. Li Bing had left complete instructions for its maintenance; his advice to "clear out the beds and keep the dykes and spillways low" has been heeded. Ensuing generations have followed the rules of river control inscribed at Li Erlang's temple that read, in part; "Respect the ancient system. And do not lightly modify it." ∎

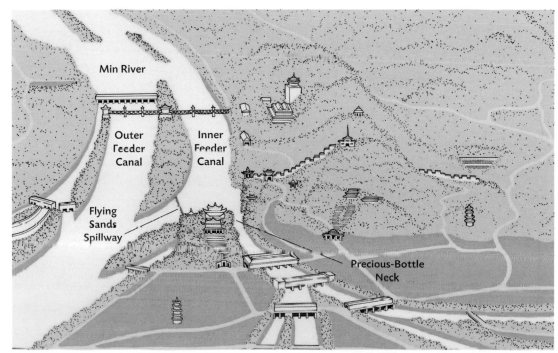

THE THAMES BARRIER: The Thames Barrier, a pier-and-gate structure in the river's channel eight miles downstream from London, stands at the ready to forestall disaster. With surge tides threatening and—over the long term—southeast England sinking and ocean levels rising, all factors point to inevitable flooding that would devastate a 45-square-mile floodplain where almost two million people live.

A 1953 tidal surge that inundated parts of London and killed 300 people downstream spurred

Right: Each of the steel-clad shells houses a giant rocker beam that rotates the gate-closing mechanism.

Below: The barrier's gates operate on the same principle as a gas cock. As shown in the diagram, open gates allow water through; when closed, they shut off the flow.

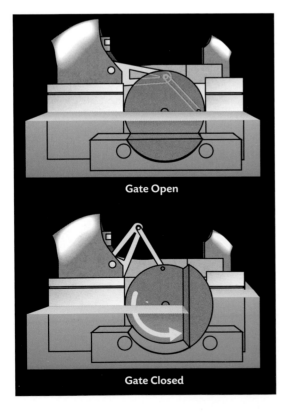

Gate Open

Gate Closed

construction of the Thames barrier. Designed by the engineering firm of Rendel, Palmer & Tritton, the complex structure includes ten rotating steel gates spanning the 1,700-foot-wide channel at Woolwich. Flush with the riverbed when open, the gates rotate 90 degrees to a height of 60 feet when closed, an operation that takes less than a half hour. The gates are separated by nine enormous piers topped with steel-

clad shells *(above)* housing machinery that operates the gates.

In 1974, an Anglo-Dutch consortium began construction of the barrier in sections, which allowed river traffic to continue. Cofferdams created dry areas for building the six-story piers with their mazes of passageways, gate-support structures, and controls. The 10,000-ton concrete sills that support the gates were cast on-site, floated out into the channel, and lowered into place. A Liverpool company fabricated the shells of laminated wood clad with stainless steel and transported them to their Woolwich destination.

Costing more than half a billion dollars, the Thames Barrier project was completed in 1984. Already experts are looking ahead some 50 years, when rising tides could exceed the barrier's height. ■

THE DUTCH SEA BARRIER: The Dutch have always battled the sea. One-fourth of the land is below sea level, and more than half is prone to twice-daily flooding by normal tides. Centuries ago the Dutch built their homes on artificial mounds above the sea's reach. Later, they used windmills to drain the land and constructed dikes and dams to restrain the tides, but these devices were no match for severe North Sea storms.

A savage storm tide in 1953 inundated the southwestern delta region, killing thousands and prompting the country to undertake the world's most ambitious and sophisticated flood protection project. Known as

Thirty-one gates span the two northern channels of the Oosterschelde barrier. For the time being, Dutch engineers have tamed—but not conquered—the North Sea.

the Deltaplan, or Delta Project, it includes four large dams between the Westerschelde and the New Waterway. Its eight-year final phase, completed in 1986, involved the construction of a two-mile-long surge barrier in the Oosterschelde estuary.

Many technical problems had to be solved. The Dutch built several work harbors for transfer and storage of construction materials, as well as work sites on three artificial islands built on sandbars in the estuary itself. Two of the islands were then connected by a

Opposite: **Giant mattresses to stabilize the seabed of the Oosterschelde estuary unroll like paper towels from the construction vessel *Cardium*. Preparing the seafloor was the first step in building the open surge barrier.**

dam. This left the estuary permanently divided into three channels, each to receive a section of the surge barrier. Central to the design are 65 gigantic concrete piers that support the 400-ton steel gates, their hydraulic lifting mechanisms, and the massive sills and beams that stabilize the whole structure, as well as the roadway that caps the barrier.

The plan's hoisting and transport needs exceeded the capabilities of existing cranes, and so five different vessels *(below)* were designed for specialized tasks. As one engineer put it, "We had to invent everything from scratch, including a technique for stabilizing the seabed."

Today, engineers often test the barrier gates. Thirty-one operating strategies can respond to any kind of storm. In spring 1990, when put to the test, the surge barrier passed with flying colors and should protect the Netherlands for centuries to come. ∎

Below: **New concepts in dam design and a fleet of specialized vessels made the sea barrier possible. Many elements provide a firm base for the movable gates that regulate tidal flow in the estuary. Stabilizing mattresses support sand-ballasted concrete piers; an armor layer of large rocks provides additional weight. Sills and beams define openings for the 400-ton gates, while a duct in the roadway beam houses hydraulic and electronic equipment.**

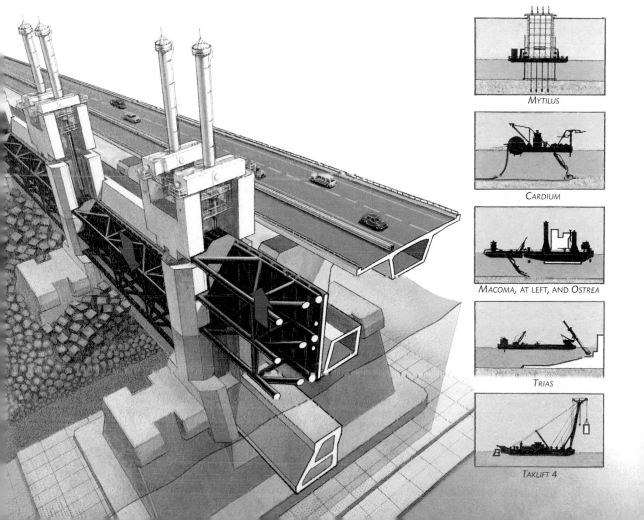

MYTILUS

CARDIUM

MACOMA, AT LEFT, AND OSTREA

TRIAS

TAKLIFT 4

TO THE SPIRIT

Pyramids
Temples
Domes
Gothic Cathedrals

HUMANS HAVE LONG MADE STRUCTURES that stretch the fabric of belief into palpable form, whether as places of worship, strongholds of god-kings, tombs, or observatories to probe the cosmos.

Historically, the quest for the eternal accounts for a great number of the advances that have been seen in building technology. Religion's central role in most civilizations usually ensured vast expenditures of resources, manpower, and talent on these structures.

Many of the great monuments of ancient societies still elude understanding. How were 50-ton sarsens transported to Stonehenge? And why? What did the blue stones signify? Across the Atlantic, Spanish conquistadores concluded that the 200-ton blocks at one Inca site had been positioned by magic. Huge monuments built without the use of wheels or pulleys might suggest the intervention of supernatural forces to some, but the builders labored mightily to link heaven and earth. Egypt's greatest pyramids symbolized not only pharaonic power but also celestial stairways; Sumerian ziggurats, visible 25 miles away, were "hills of heaven."

In addition to overcoming logistical obstacles, builders of such monuments solved basic construction problems. Recesses and buttresses alternately lightened and reinforced the mud-brick ziggurats, for example. Far more advanced, the Pyramids at Giza employed corbeling to deflect the downward thrust of thousands of tons of limestone from the internal passages and burial chambers.

As freestanding temples evolved, they usually took the simplest of structural forms, beams and columns. The gleaming marble temples dating to Greece's Golden Age derived from simpler timber structures. But on a large scale, unreinforced masonry couldn't bear up to the tensile stresses of beam-and-post construction.

Masonry could be extended over huge spaces, though, if curved. Roman builders created the masonry dome, among the most versatile of spanning structures. The Romans employed local materials such as volcanic rock and sand to make their supple concrete. The pride of an empire at its peak was reflected in the great dome of the Pantheon, the largest in the world until modern times. ■

Preceding pages: Roughly contemporaneous with the Giza pyramids, Stonehenge appears to share much more with classical Greek temples, especially in its post-and-lintel construction.

Left: Reims Cathedral, Haute Marne, France

Opposite: **Although at one time the Meidum Pyramid was converted from a stepped pyramid to a true pyramid, its limestone sheath was later removed.**

Pyramids

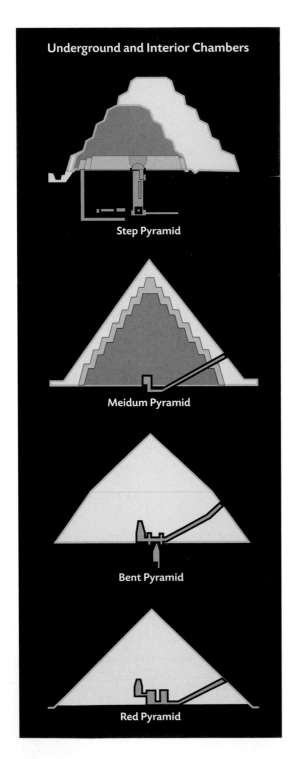

Underground and Interior Chambers

Step Pyramid

Meidum Pyramid

Bent Pyramid

Red Pyramid

EGYPT'S LARGEST PYRAMIDS are the most massive monuments ever built. More than by their scale, however, the pyramids awe by their implausibility. Most were built between 2700 and 2100 B.C. by a civilization that labored without benefit of the wheel, the pulley, or a metal tougher than copper.

Tombs for the Old Kingdom's pharaohs, the pyramids may also have served as temples to the sun god Ra. They were also vast public works projects that employed hundreds of thousands of conscripted farmers idled by the Nile's seasonal flooding.

Benchlike mastabas and other brick-covered royal tombs of the Early Dynastic period (circa 2920-2575 B.C.) signal the pyramid's origin. These tombs evolved from simple earthen mounds covering crude burial pits into squared-off structures of sunbaked brick concealing elaborate underground compartments.

But nothing that came before it compared with the tomb built about 2630 B.C. in Saqqara for the pharaoh Djoser by his chancellor and architect, Imhotep. Over a subterranean warren of chambers and passageways, Imhotep set a solid, square mastaba. Then Imhotep began tinkering with his creation, enlarging it and building it higher until it was some 200 feet tall, with a 400-by-350-foot base. Courses of rock laid atop the structure radically changed it. No longer a mastaba, the limestone-cased Step Pyramid introduced a new structural shape.

Other important changes occurred: The Step Pyramid was built of small stone blocks. But for the pyramids at Meidum and Dashûr, huge blocks were quarried and dragged on sledges to building sites. With time and trial, the builders also became adept at corbeling—building false arches and vaults by overhanging each successive layer of stone inward over the one below it until two sides meet. ■

THE GREAT PYRAMID: Sole surviving wonders of the ancient world, the Great Pyramid of Khufu and those of his successors Khafre and Menkaure at Giza remain structurally intact, with the Khafre Pyramid retaining its smooth limestone facing near the top.

Scholars theorize that by the beginning of the reign of Khufu, about 2551 B.C., the ascendancy of the sun cult of Heliopolis had heightened the pyramid's symbolic importance: It reproduced in stone the sunbursts that projected pyramids of light across the Nile.

The rapid evolution of the pyramid under Khufu's father, Snefru, gave the Egyptians the practical experience to build large pyramids penetrated by intricate internal structures and to undertake construction at what became the ideal 51°52' slope. Still, Khufu's monument involved mind-boggling leaps of scale: From a base covering 13.1 acres, the Great Pyramid soared 481 feet (about 30 feet have since been lost), its 2.3 million stone blocks averaging 2.5 tons each. ▪

Left: **Sited on a rise, Khafre's pyramid** *(center)* **only appears larger than Khufu's** *(background),* **which reaches between 400 and 500 feet.**

Above: To deflect the load of 400 feet of stone above it, the burial chamber was buffered with five chambers. Four have flat roofs; the topmost has a pointed saddle roof that redirects downward thrust into side walls.

TEMPLE OF THE INSCRIPTIONS: Set atop a truncated pyramid at the Mayan archaeological site at Palenque, in Mexico, the Temple of the Inscriptions originally towered over the surrounding forest, a reminder to all that the gods were ever present. The secret of the temple was not discovered until the 1950s when a hidden stairway was discovered beneath the temple floor. The twisting passageway led down through the interior of the pyramid to a crypt covered by a huge stone slab housing the tomb of a famous ruler and jade treasure.

Opposite: **Massive columns rise in the Hypostyle Hall of the great temple complex at Karnak, Egypt, which was erected about 1300 B.C.**

Temples

SINCE ANCIENT TIMES, societies have sought to understand and to live in harmony with the universe. Many of their structures reflect this age-old quest.

The great ziggurat at Ur, in present-day Iraq, suggests the cosmic mountain central to ancient Middle Eastern mythology. Brick facings eight feet thick sheathe the mud-brick core. Three tiers draw the eye upward to the terrace, once the site of a temple sacred to the moon god, Nanna.

The sitting of the great stone circle at Stonehenge, in England, testifies to the importance of celestial events—such as the summer solstice—in the lives of early agricultural people.

In Nara, Japan, eighth-century builders tested the limits of timber-frame construction to house the world's largest bronze statue of Buddha in the great hall of the Todaiji temple complex. Thus they conveyed the enormous spiritual impact of Buddhism on their culture.

Temple builders responded to the need for spiritual expression not only with structures constructed on a massive scale, but also with works of beauty that existed in harmony with the natural surroundings. They pushed their skills to the utmost to create structures that were meant to last. Dedicated to the worship of gods, such buildings were worthy of the finest work and the best technology that builders everywhere could offer. ■

Below: **Reconstructed ziggurat at Ur, built about 2100 B.C.**

THE PARTHENON: The best known Greek temples were built in the period between the defeat of the Persians in 480 B.C. and the death of Alexander the Great in 323 B.C. Perhaps the most famous temple is the Parthenon, which incorporates refinements in structure and design commonly used in fifth-century Athens.

The elegance of Greek temples was achieved through subtle, lucid design. Stability depended on sturdy underpinning. Builders normally carried a foundation of carefully coursed masonry—usually made of limestone—down to bedrock, often to a depth of many feet. On this rested a platform made up of three or four courses of marble, held together in both the horizontal and vertical planes by iron dowels embedded in lead. Such construction was resistant to the earthquakes that occasionally shake this seismically active region.

The masonry of the Parthenon, like that of other ancient Greek buildings, was laid without mortar. As shown in the diagram at bottom right, individual columns were usually constructed of a series of drum-like units centered by socketed dowels. After the drums were carefully joined together, the surface of the column was channeled by master carvers. ■

Far right: **A masterpiece of engineering and architecture as well, the Greek Parthenon has withstood earthquakes and wars. The elegant temple is essentially a simple structure of vertical supports and horizontal top and bottom stones.**

Right top: **Columns of Doric temples such as the Parthenon stand on a platform of stone slabs resting on a deep stone foundation. The capital transmits the load of stone above it to the shaft for conveyance to the platform and into the earth.**

Right bottom: **The drumlike units of a column.**

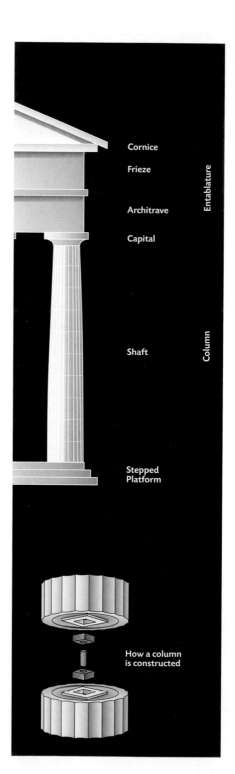

Cornice

Frieze

Architrave

Capital

Entablature

Shaft

Column

Stepped Platform

How a column is constructed

CHINESE TIMBER-FRAMING: China, like Greece, endures frequent earthquakes, and centuries of experience led its engineers to take seismic activity into account. To counter horizontal movements, they devised flexible structures that relied on the integrity of their framework. The principal building material was timber, and woods with excellent tensile strength, such as cedar, were highly prized.

Architecture entered a glorious age during the Song dynasty (A.D. 960-1279). Builders used a system of construction developed centuries earlier and based on time-tested rules. These rules, along with other specialized data, were published in A.D. 1103.

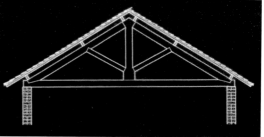

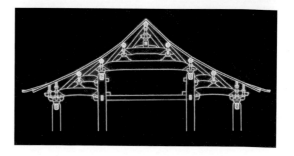

Buddha images gaze in the four directions *(left)* on an upper level of China's Yingxian Pagoda. Earthquakes, floods, and human violence have left their marks on the 11th-century temple *(below)*, but its sturdy frame still stands firm today.

Song officials used the *Yingzao fashi* (Building Standards) to determine design and structural requirements and to estimate material and labor needs.

In typical structures, a raised platform rested on a tamped-earth foundation. The platform formed the base for a timber post-and-lintel frame, which supported a series of brackets that in turn supported a pitched roof with overhanging eaves. The overall layout of a building was determined by the number and placement of modular units called *jian*, or bays. Such a modular system facilitates prefabrication.

Opposite. In conventional Western architecture, a triangular truss dictates the straight pitch of the roof *(top)*. In China, as a timber skeleton of columns and beams rises toward the ridge *(bottom)*, a series of graduated steps underlies the purlins and rafters supporting the roof.

The roof was the most striking feature. For protection against the elements, it extended well beyond the building's foundation. The traditional Chinese builder could produce a roof of any size and curvature simply by manipulating the lengths and widths of posts and crossbeams in the timber skeleton rising toward the ridge.

Built in 1056, the Yingxian Pagoda in the northern province of Shanxi is China's oldest surviving pagoda built entirely of wood. Its multiple levels of wooden bracing interlock to give stability.

The ingenious Chinese system greatly influenced building practices in a vast area of Asia. Japan's Hall of the Great Buddha in Nara, for example, was inspired by Chinese structures. Timber-framing is still carried on in parts of Asia today. ▪

OBSERVATORIES: For millennia, the authority to rule was linked with the ability to foretell the future. Power accrued to those who could predict eclipses, phases of the moon, the reappearance of certain stars, and the winter and summer solstices and who knew the proper days for performing rituals, waging war, and planting and harvesting.

To have such knowledge required making regular celestial observations and carefully recording them. Before the development of the telescope, sighting techniques relied on the naked eye. Often, observers were aided by structures or instruments of considerable size. These sighting aids might have a solar orientation or celestial alignments with doorways, windows, or markers.

A medieval stargazer, Prince Ulugh Beg of Turkestan, built an observatory in Samarkand that was considered a wonder of the world. One of his measuring devices was said to rival Hagia Sophia in height.

In 18th-century India, Prince Jai Singh II constructed an observatory at Jaipur that held about a dozen stone instruments, including an enormous sundial. The sundial's 90-foot gnomon has a hypotenuse paralleling the Earth's axis. On each side is a quadrant of a circle, paralleling the plane of the Equator. At sunrise the gnomon's shadow falls on the highest point of the western quadrant; it descends until noon, then ascends the eastern quadrant.

Such simple masonry instruments provided sufficient data until relatively recent times, when they gave way to the exquisite precision of modern telescopes and atomic clocks. ∎

Opposite: **At the 18th-century observatory in Jaipur, India, the shadow cast by the gnomon of a gigantic sundial on quadrants of a circle permits observers to track the sun's movement and thus determine time of day.**

Above: **Unlike the modern observatories it resembles, this temple at Chichen Itza in Yucatán housed no scientific instruments; it honored a Maya god. Windowlike openings align with the setting sun at the equinoxes and with Venus, the planet associated with war and death.**

Below: **Stonehenge's solar orientation would have made it easy for priests to pinpoint the solstices and to plan ceremonies connected with the passage of the seasons.**

Domes

DOMES ANSWER THE CHALLENGE of enclosing large spaces without the use of internal supports. For almost 2,000 years, domes have held the record for spanning the greatest interior spaces. For longer, they have curved over mounds, tombs, and small temples. Igloos, hogans, and yurts still depend on the form, created by rotating an arch around a vertical axis and providing continuous support along the perimeter.

In domes, structural forces exert powerful outward thrusts that prevented early builders from doming any but the most basic of freestanding structures. Undaunted, Roman builders freed the dome from its humble past by using concrete, composed of high-grade cement with aggregates of stone and brick fragments. By the second century A.D., concrete had superseded brick and stone.

The Romans left a few problems for later builders. Byzantine architects perfected a method for placing domes atop square or rectangular structures. In his Renaissance design for the cupola of the Florence Duomo, Filippo Brunelleschi divided the dome into inner and outer shells. Lighter, stronger materials—cast iron, reinforced concrete, steel, inflatable man-made fabrics—and advances in physics have simplified dome building. Today's huge domes, such as the Superdome in New Orleans, are monuments to secular society. ■

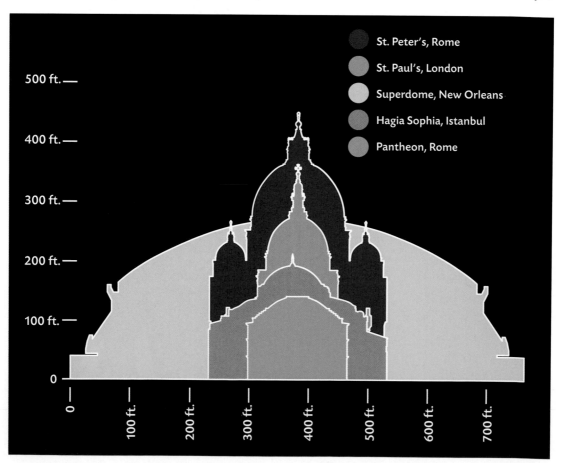

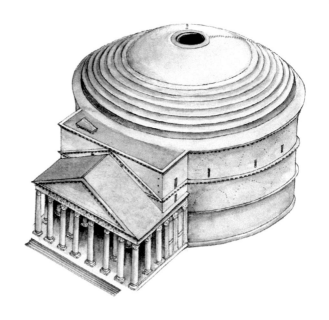

THE PANTHEON: Dedicated in its day to "all the gods," the Pantheon today honors an unknown Roman architect whose vision created one of the most influential buildings of any era. Structural soundness and its consecration as a church in 609 have combined to keep the Pantheon in use for nearly 1,900 years.

The dome of the emperor Hadrian's new structure, begun in 118 and completed a decade later, demanded a formidable support system. Possibly building on the site of an earlier temple, workers began with a 24-foot-wide circular foundation wall. Above it, they built 20-foot-thick support walls—effectively a cylinder to contain the dome's outward thrust. Though thick, the encapsulating walls are riddled with voids; inside them, a complex web of vaults

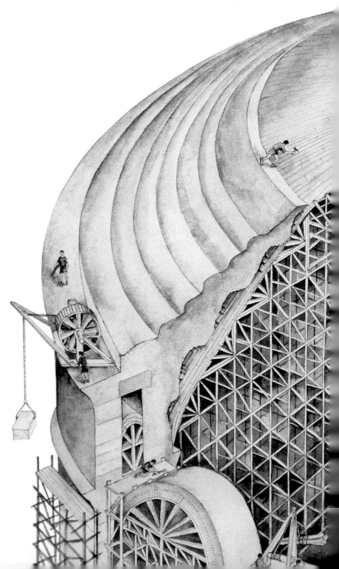

Above: Two levels of large brick barrel vaults channel the dome's load to piers below—and show the complex construction of the walls.

Opposite: **Overlapping layers of concrete create concentric stepped rings that thicken the dome's base, as in Roman arch construction, and lessen stress.**

and arches channels the vertical load from the dome down to eight massive piers. At the crown of the dome, the monolithic shell tapers to 59 inches thick.

Though chunky compared with the modern, machine-mixed variety, Roman concrete was so supple that, when wet, it could be curved and shaped at will over formwork. Cemented by excellent mortars of volcanic sand, it contained varying mixes of aggregates: stone, volcanic rock, brick, even rubble from demolished buildings. These allowed builders to modulate the density of their structures. Rising layer by horizontal layer, the Pantheon's concrete lightens, reducing loadings in the material to roughly half that of heavier aggregates. The dome culminates in a 27-foot open oculus, or eye, lined with brick and sheathed in gilded bronze, which suggests the truest legacy of its architect: making the inside, not the outside, of the building the focus of attention. ■

The dome may have taken shape over timber formwork, as in the cutaway at left. On the dome's interior, five rings of square coffers in a wafflelike pattern, diminishing in size and depth, create illusions of space.

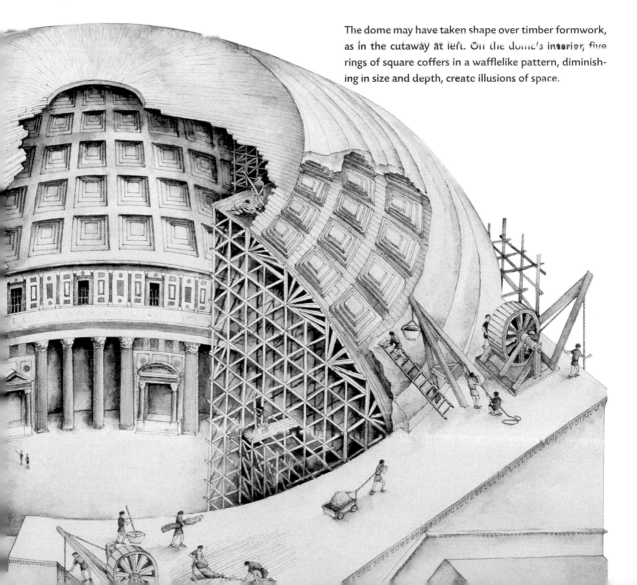

Above: **Billowing semidomes at east and west provide partial support for the central dome. Buttresses north and south foreshadow Gothic architecture.**

HAGIA SOPHIA: The greatest of Byzantium's domed structures and for nine centuries the world's largest church, Hagia Sophia reflects an empire at its height and an emperor, Justinian, who pushed monumental building arts to new limits. Hagia Sophia's chief designers were Anthemius of Tralles, a geometer, and Isidorus of Miletus, a natural scientist. Both devised daring solutions to Hagia Sophia's unique building challenges. For instance, the necklace of windows that helps create the illusion of a "suspended" dome is an expedient to prevent meridional cracks.

Early churches took two distinct forms: the rectangular basilica and the round, domed building. Justinian handed Anthemius and Isidorus the formidable task of wedding the two forms into a kind of domed basilica. The building's overall floor plan encloses a rectangle some 220 by 300 feet.

Substantial deformations of the main piers occurred even before the arches were completed. The architects strengthened the massive mortared-brick buttresses outside Hagia Sophia's north and south walls, but this didn't prevent the dome's collapse in 558, after two earthquakes. The dome that replaced it was 20 feet higher, soaring to some 180 feet. The second dome has also suffered partial collapses after earthquakes but remains essentially in its original form. ■

Opposite: **As ethereal inside as it is massively material outside, Hagia Sophia depends on a well-concealed support system. Colonnaded aisles and galleries are carefully integrated into the open, light-filled plan.**

SAINT PETER'S BASILICA: Appointed *capo-maestro,* or chief architect, for Rome's new St. Peter's Basilica in 1546, the 71-year-old Michelangelo inherited the project from illustrious predecessors, among them Bramante and Raphael.

Michelangelo redesigned the dome with Brunelleschi's Florence masterpiece in mind. After his own death in 1564, only the drum was complete; when finished nearly three decades later, the dome, though altered, still reflected his mastery.

Directly over what many believe to be St. Peter's tomb, the double-vaulted brick dome rises to 452 feet at the top of its cross. The dome's diameter, 137 feet, is essentially the same as that of Florence. Four great piers, more than 60 feet wide, anchor its arches. Pendentives form a transition between the arches and the dome's circular drum. To counter hoop tension in the dome, caused by its tendency to expand, the builders wrapped two iron chains around it.

But neither chains nor the steep dome's lower supporting structures were sufficient to contain outward thrusts. As a result, after a century and a half, the ribbed dome had cracked badly, threatening to split open. In 1742, Giovanni Poleni, a professor of "experimental philosophy," was called in by Pope Benedict XIV to consult. His pioneering application of structural mechanics to an architectural problem resulted in five more iron chains being wreathed around the dome. But Poleni also determined that the vertical cracks that segmented the dome into many arches posed no potential danger.

Rows of windows pierce 16 ribbed compartments as they curve toward the lantern. Though no longer visible from everywhere in Rome, as Michelangelo intended, the lead-sheathed dome still dominates the exterior of this tallest of all Renaissance churches.

ST PAUL'S CATHEDRAL: London's Great Fire of 1666 claimed 87 churches, among them Old St. Paul's Cathedral, the stones of which, said one diarist, "flew like granados [grenades], the melting lead running down the streets in a stream and the very pavements glowing with fiery redness." On orders of King Charles II, St. Paul's was rebuilt by Sir Christopher Wren.

The most dramatic aspect of St. Paul's is its great dome, second in size only to that of St. Peter's Basilica in Rome. An admirer of St. Peter's and its double dome, Wren was alarmed by that structure's cracking. In addition, the rubble-filled piers of the new St. Paul's had started to spall, or break up, even before the dome design was in hand. These conditions demanded unprecedented lightness.

Wren achieved this by using three distinct structures: a lightweight inner, hemispherical dome of brick only 18 inches thick; a central brick cone also 18 inches thick, bearing at its top 365 feet above the pavement an 850-ton lantern; and an outer shell of lead-sheathed timber. A single iron chain resists spreading forces throughout the system.

The cone has a small oculus at its top. Below this aperture is an oculus that is considerably larger. Light enters the upper oculus indirectly, through gaps in the outer dome. The larger aperture gives the illusion, however, that St Paul's is flooded with light.

The cone is an inverted catenary, the optimal state for a thin, load-bearing structure. Wren's cone is further stabilized and compressed by the lantern, based on Filippo Brunelleschi's design for Florence's Santa Maria del Fiore Cathedral, and reinforced by the chain at its base. These forces prevent the hoop tension—the tension found around the lower part of a dome—that plagues St. Peter's and other great domes.

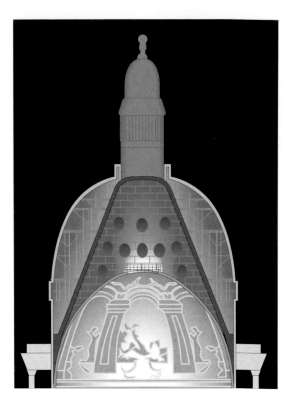

Above: **Catenary principles, developed by mathematician Robert Hooke, guided Wren to build his brick cone. The shape adopted by a chain hanging from two points, a catenary exerts entirely tensile, or pulling, force. But the same shape turned upside down is compressive.**

Opposite: **Skin-deep resemblance to St. Peter's outer and inner domes, which Wren never actually saw, stops at the structural level. The colonnaded drum is reminiscent; St. Paul's holds 32 buttresses and intercolumnar reinforcing walls. Within the basilica, eight piers and four towerlike bastions are joined together by a series of arches and barrel vaults.**

During construction of the dome, Wren checked on its progress two or three times a week by being hoisted up in a basket and was thus able to see, when work was completed in 1708, as his son positioned the last bit of Portland stone on the lantern.

When Wren died in 1723 he was honored by becoming the first person to be buried in St. Paul's. The inscription on his tomb in the cathedral crypt translates from the Latin as "Reader, if you seek his memorial, look about you." ■

SAINT ISAAC'S DOME: Saints and angels surround the Virgin Mary in St. Isaac's dome in St. Petersburg, Russia. Completed in 1842, the cast-iron dome became a model for others, including the U.S. Capitol's, which is the world's largest iron dome.

Opposite: **At Amiens soaring, repetitive vertical elements unite to evoke the sublime.**

Gothic Cathedrals

THE FLOWERING OF THE HIGH MIDDLE AGES in France, from the mid-12th through the 13th centuries, was made possible by merchant wealth, religious fervor, and labor's organization into specialized crafts.

In 1144, the completion of a new choir for the abbey church of St. Denis that incorporated ribbed vaulting and large stained-glass windows signaled the birth of the revolutionary new Gothic style. Abbot Suger, who commissioned the choir, believed in the spiritual power of light, and the quest for that light became the cathedral builders' greatest challenge.

Armed only with simple tools and geometric relationships, master masons formed high, pointed vaults and integrated them with a system of flying buttresses. Gothic cathedrals soon rose to unheard-of heights,

Below: **As towns vied for prestige, cathedrals rose higher.**

and their radiant great rose windows became the emblems of the age.

Also busy at the cathedral site were craftsmen skilled in making and piecing together the brilliantly colored glass to fill the stone outlines of the enormous windows. In large earthen pots, the glassmakers mixed metal oxides with molten glass to obtain jewel-like colors: cobalt for blue, copper for red and green, and manganese for purple. The glass was often blown and worked into a cylindrical shape; then, once it had cooled, the glazier used a hot iron to cut it into the proper shapes and sizes—usually smaller than the palm of his hand. The details of the windows' sacred scenes were painted on with opaque enamel, which was then fired to fuse it completely to the glass. The whole translucent puzzle was supported by ironwork and held together with strips of lead. ∎

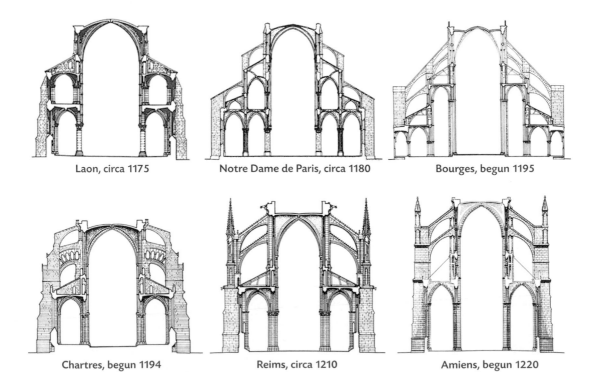

Laon, circa 1175

Notre Dame de Paris, circa 1180

Bourges, begun 1195

Chartres, begun 1194

Reims, circa 1210

Amiens, begun 1220

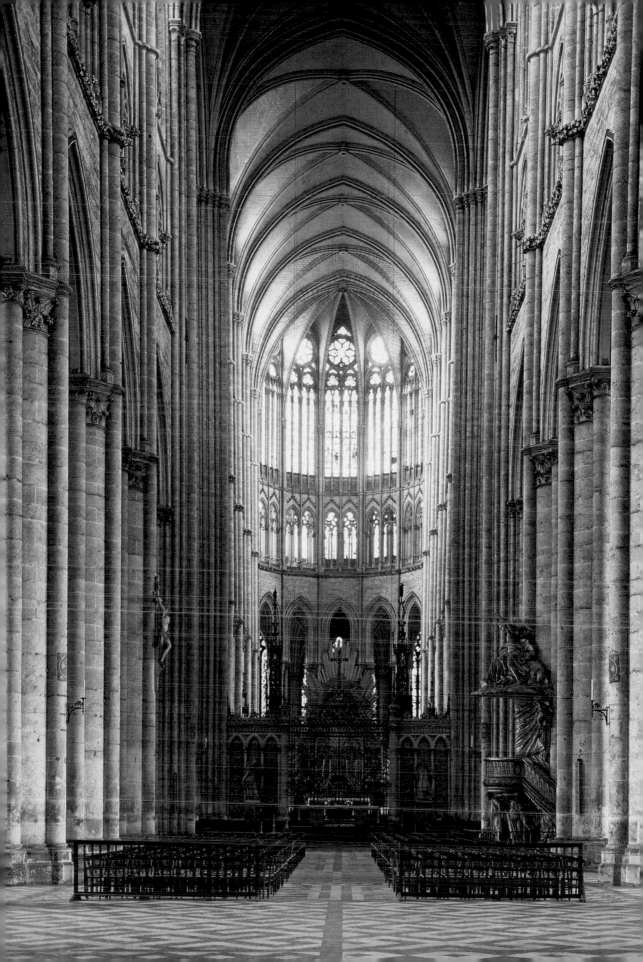

NOTRE DAME DE PARIS: Begun around 1150, Notre Dame was planned from the outset to be a quarter taller than its tallest predecessor. The building is also notable for the introduction, around 1180, of flying buttresses, which propped up the upper walls and braced them against the lateral thrust of the vaults and against a heavy wind load. They were immediately adopted at other sites.

Notre Dame's glory, however, was its great rayonnant, or radiating, geometric rose windows. Freed of bearing loads, walls were opened to a tremendous diameter. So perfect was the design of the north rose that its stone fillet has supported 1,300 square feet of glass for 700 years. The skill involved was so precise that fewer than 20 of these windows were attempted in France in a hundred years—and none surpasses Notre Dame's in size.

Below: Pointed, ribbed quadripartite vaulting helped to further the aims of the builders of Gothic cathedrals. The vault consisted of a thin skin laid over strong ribs. Slender columns served to carry its weight.

The pointed Gothic arch allowed more flexibility than the semicircular Romanesque arch, and Gothic vaulting was much lighter. Once the flying buttress was introduced at Notre Dame, walls could be opened with larger and more dazzling windows.

BUILDING GOTHIC CATHEDRALS: At the height of activity, the construction site of a Gothic cathedral swarmed with dozens of workmen, just like any high-rise building site today.

Members of craft guilds, the contracted workmen were organized into job teams and, unlike serfs, were paid for their labor. This organization of the work site remains perhaps the most modern achievement. Using simple hand tools (triangle and compass, plumb bob and square, metal ax and chisel, winch, carpenter's plane) and one new labor-saving device, the wheelbarrow, the cathedral builders realized the most complex industrial projects undertaken in Europe since Roman times.

Each site was supervised by a master mason, a master carpenter, and perhaps as many as 30 senior craftsmen. These specialists and some of their more skilled workers moved from job to job, applying lessons learned on one to the next.

Gothic engineering was not a science in the modern sense, but more an art. The master mason served as designer, artist, and craftsman, like those who worked under him. Armed with a level, a square, a triangle, a straight edge, measuring rods and strings, and a compass, he set the plan for the cathedral.

Second only to the master mason in authority, the master carpenter designed and supervised the construction of the all-important temporary scaffolding, including the heavy, braced centering frames that supported the arches and the ribs of the vault until the keystones were set and the arches complete.

The master carpenter also knew geometry; his centering gave physical form to the master mason's geometrical planning, creating the exact angle and curve of every arch.

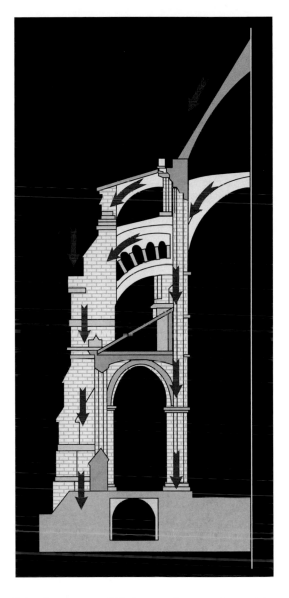

Flying buttresses, which bear against massive upright buttresses along the church's perimeter, restrain the outward thrust of the vaults and direct it downward, freeing the walls from carrying the load.

Building design must have been worked out in drawings or small-scale models. Once the floor plan had been established, the builders worked out full-scale details geometrically on a plaster floor known as a tracing floor. To minimize costs and to avoid massive reconstruction if design problems occurred, the superstructure was often built one bay at a time. ∎

Wind
Solar
Hydroelectric

ALONE IN A LANDSCAPE of pasture or polder, a windmill looks like a quaint anachronism—an evocation of a bygone era when wind supplied a deceptively simple solution, mechanical power, to the problems of pumping water and grinding grain. The modern windmill, however, is a wind turbine, which converts wind energy into electricity.

The search for renewable sources of energy that address the world's growing demands without compromising the environment is one of the modern world's most compelling challenges. Most of the energy in use today still comes from highly polluting, nonrenewable fossil fuels. Nuclear energy is also a resource, but nuclear power plants generate radioactive wastes, and even the safest of them carry inherent risks.

In addition to wind, the most promising alternative energy sources are water and sunlight—the most reliable and renewable of all energies. In all three cases, the resource must be readily available; thus, siting is important. Wind turbines are most productive in windy areas; solar thermal plants work best in sunny, semiarid regions; hydroelectric dams are practical only where water is plentiful.

The economical operation of wind turbines is possible only in areas with annual average winds of at least 12 miles an hour. Although California generates most of the world's wind power, more wind actually blows over the strip of states from North Dakota to Texas—giving them even greater potential wind resources.

Solar energy can be converted into electricity using two systems: solar thermal and photovoltaic. In solar thermal systems, receiving units capture the sun's heat and convert it into steam, which can be used to power electric generators. Photovoltaic systems rely instead on solar cells that convert light directly into electricity.

For all their promise, alternative energy systems are not without problems, most notably the need for practical yet inexpensive ways to store electricity for times when power plants are idled by lack of wind, sunshine, or water. Even so, the benefits of these systems are enormous: a lessened dependence on fossil fuels and a reduced threat to the environment. ∎

Preceding pages: Wind turbines spin like pinwheels at California's Tehachapi Pass. Sited to catch currents entering the Mojave Desert, the turbines form a vast California network.

Left: The 148-foot-high parabolic mirror of France's Odeillo Solar Furnace works like a magnifying lens to concentrate sunlight, focusing it on a small intensely hot area.

Opposite: Danish-built wind turbines, modern-day counterparts of the old-fashioned windmill, sweep halos on the horizon in California's Altamont Pass.

Wind

WIND IS A FORM OF SOLAR ENERGY, the result of the uneven heating of the Earth's surface and the effects of its rotation. Wind is also an energy source in itself.

The earliest known attempt to snare the wind and tap its power by means of a windmill dates to seventh-century Persia. In 13th-century Europe, two kinds of windmills evolved: a post mill whose sails, attached to a horizontal beam, turned on a central vertical post to face the wind, and a tower mill whose sails were mounted on a rotating "cap." Such models were widely adapted.

Today, more than 18,000 wind turbines operate in the U.S. The majority are in California, where most of the world's wind-generated electricity is produced at a low cost both to the consumer and the environment. ▪

Drawing of extant windmill in New York dates to 1806.

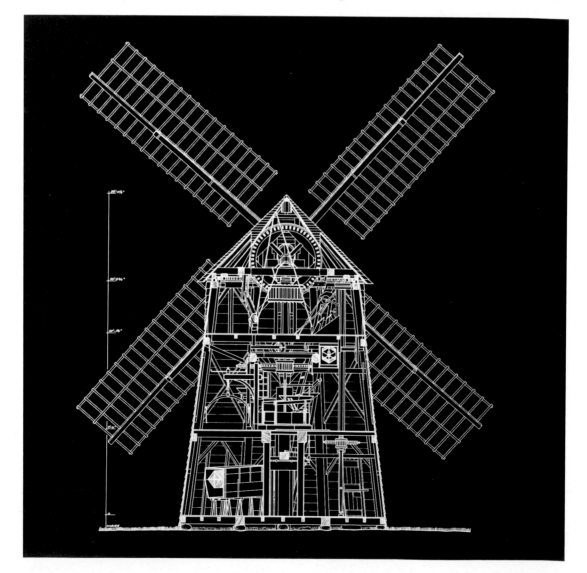

Solar

ALTHOUGH IT IS 93 MILLION MILES AWAY, the sun is Earth's single most important source of energy. In fact, the solar energy that makes its way to Earth in one minute is more than the total amount of energy used by the planet's entire population in one year. The problem, of course, is that the sun's energy must be collected, concentrated, stored, and converted into other, more usable forms of energy.

Collecting and concentrating the sun's rays is as simple as holding a magnifying glass to the sun. Converting solar radiation into electricity is more complex.

Solar thermal systems use refective surfaces, such as U-shaped troughs, concave parabolic dishes, and flat mirrors (called heliostats). These surfaces direct sunlight into receivers that produce heat, which can be used to make high-pressure steam to turn electric generators.

In facilities using a central-receiver configuration, heliostats focus sunlight onto a centrally located tower. Fluid in a receiver atop the tower is heated and transferred to an energy-conversion unit at the tower's base. In trough collectors, sunlight heats a fluid-filled tube along the trough's axis, whereas in parabolic dishes, the receiver is mounted above the center of the dish. Solar heat can also be used for manufacturing and might be useful in destroying wastes created by older technologies. ■

Below: **California's Solar One**

CARRIZO PLAIN: The photovoltaic effect was first recognized in 1839, when French physicist Antoine-César Becquerel discovered that certain materials produce an electric current when light strikes them. This realization led to the development of photovoltaic, or solar, cells.

Solar cells are made from purified silicon and other semiconducting materials. As the cell absorbs light, it releases electrons that flow through an external circuit, producing an electric current.

Primitive devices, the first solar cells converted light to electricity with only a one percent efficiency rate. Today's commercial cells have efficiency rates that are as great as 14 percent. Laboratory rates are twice that.

Cells are usually grouped into modules, which are then assembled into arrays. The simplest array uses flat-plate modules. Typically, these have a transparent cover, front or back structural supports, and layers of laminates to encapsulate the solar cells.

Photovoltaic systems are quiet, require no fuel, and generate no pollution. They are lightweight and portable. The U.S. space program first used one in 1958 to power a satellite's radio. Today, small systems power calculators and watches, while larger ones light highways and homes.

Some provide power to utility grids. The largest, on California's Carrizo Plain, was built in 1984. Though since decommissioned, it supplied data for designing the next generation of large utility systems now in operation around the country. ∎

Clouds and sky are mirrored in the reflector panels that bracket each bank of solar cells on California's Carrizo Plain. Both the cells and their reflector panels are mounted on a two-axis tracker designed to keep the photovoltaic array precisely oriented toward the sun.

Opposite: Rising more than 70 stories from bedrock, Glen Canyon Dam's concrete arch holds back the Colorado River in Arizona.

Hydroelectric

FEW STRUCTURES ARE HIGHER and none are heavier than dams; among the highest and heaviest dams are those that trap Earth's rivers to produce electricity.

The use of water power to produce electricity for long-distance transmission began in the 1890s in the United States, with the building of a power station below Niagara Falls to supply the city of Buffalo. Theodore Roosevelt Dam in Arizona, built in 1911, was the first dam to produce hydroelectricity on a large scale. More ambitious dam projects to supply electricity and irrigation water over large areas followed.

Hoover (formerly known as Boulder) Dam, which was completed in 1936, harnessed the Colorado River to provide the American Southwest with water and electric power. A series of dams in the Pacific Northwest tapped the Columbia River for power. One of the largest dam projects in the world is the Itaipú Dam on the Paraná River between Brazil and Paraguay, which opened in 1984. The dam supplies Paraguay and much of Brazil with electricity. ■

Below: **Roosevelt Dam on Arizona's Salt River**

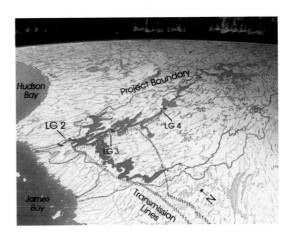

LG 2: Although western Canada is blessed with an abundance of oil and natural gas, the rest of the country is not so well endowed. Instead, eastern Canada—the province of Quebec, in particular—has more than enough water, sufficient to power one of the largest, and most controversial, hydroelectric facilities in the world today.

Begun in 1971 and still under construction, La Grande Complex embraces some 68,000 square miles of northern Quebec near James Bay—an area the size of New England. Plans call for a series of nine dams to divert several rivers into La Grande River; operating at peak capacity, the dams' powerhouses will utilize the harnessed water to generate 16,000 megawatts of electricity. The project continues to be held up, however, while the environmental impact is evaluated. ■

Above: Crown jewel of La Grande Complex, LG 2 is part of an ambitious hydroelectric project designed to power some 68,000 square miles of Quebec.

Opposite: Some 450 feet belowground, LG 2's cavernous powerhouse area took four years and almost 130,000 tons of explosives to excavate.

Below: More than 750,000 gallons of water per second cascade through LG 2's spillway and down a series of steps—a man-made cataract about three times the height of Niagara Falls.

Above: **Three long chutes (one pictured, *center*) collect surplus reservoir water, hurtling it down the quarter-mile-long spillway at speeds up to 50 miles an hour.**

THE ITAIPÚ DAM: Spanning some five miles, containing 28 million tons of concrete, and employing 40,000 workers at the peak of construction, South America's Itaipú Dam is—in the view of the president of the company that built it—"the work of the century."

Few would disagree. Indeed, Itaipú, which straddles the Paraná River along the border of Paraguay and Brazil, is one of the world's largest hydroelectric projects, its 18 generators capable of producing 12,600 megawatts of power. Not surprisingly, it was also one of the world's most expensive, costing some 18.3 billion dollars.

Construction began in 1974 with the excavation of a diversion channel to divert the Paraná River, the world's seventh largest, around the proposed dam site. To build this 1.3-mile-long channel parallel to the river

on the Brazilian side, workers over the next four years removed some 50 million tons of earth and rock. They then constructed the first section of the main dam on the new channel, after building cofferdams near its entrance and exit to keep water out of the site. Once the first section was completed, in late 1978, the cofferdams were demolished, allowing the river to flow through the diversion channel.

To ensure that the river stayed in its diversion channel while the rest of the main dam was under construction, crews erected cofferdams upstream and downstream of the main dam site and pumped dry the intervening area before excavating it to bedrock. Concrete was then poured, and the main dam and its power station gradually took shape, rising to 643 feet. At the same time, work began on the

spillway and on a buttress dam connecting the spillway to the main dam.

Although structurally complete in 1984, construction on the dam continued to 1991. Itaipú's structural bulk is matched in every way by its hydroelectric brawn. Each of the 18 generator units ensconced in the dam's cathedral-like powerhouse is fed by a 466-foot-long penstock. The generators themselves are the largest of their kind ever assembled, and each one measures 52 feet in diameter, stands 13 stories tall, and weighs an imposing 7,000 tons. Together, they provide enough electricity to meet all of Paraguay's present-day power needs and one-third of Brazil's. ■

Below: **The essential elements of the Itaipú Dam are illustrated in cross-section.**

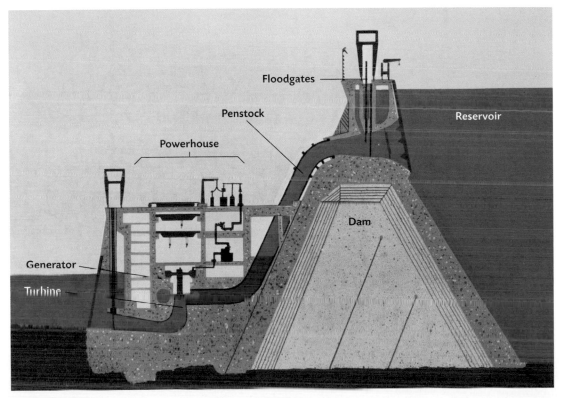

ITAIPÚ SPILLWAY: Sheltered by the exterior wall of Itaipú's spillway, two workers appear indifferent to the explosion of water and mist thundering around them. Some ten million gallons of water can surge through the spillway every second.

Glossary

Many technical terms used in *Marvels of Engineering* are explained in the text and appear in the Index. This Glossary briefly defines important terms in the context of their usage in the book.

Anchorage: a device or object that provides a secure hold, such as the huge concrete block anchoring the main cable at each end of a suspension bridge.

Aqueduct: a conduit for conveying water downhill; a structure that carries a canal over a river or valley.

Arch: a structure, typically curved, that spans an opening and supports the weight above it.

Architrave: in classical architecture, the lowest part of an entablature.

Ashlar: squared and dressed stone; masonry having a uniform pattern of horizontal and vertical joints.

Batter: to incline from the vertical; for example, the walls of some medieval castles, which recede as they rise.

Beam: a horizontal supporting member of a structure.

Bluestone: a bluish-gray building stone.

Box girder: a beam that is a hollow rectangle when viewed end-on; lighter than a solid beam.

Buttress: a projecting structure, usually of masonry, that supports or stabilizes a building or wall.

Caisson: a watertight chamber used during underwater construction work and as a foundation for a bridge pier.

Campanile: a freestanding bell tower.

Cantilever: a horizontal structural member, such as a beam, girder, or truss, that projects from a supporting column or wall.

Capital: the top part of a column.

Cast iron: a mixture of iron, carbon, and silicon cast in a mold and used to make structural parts that are hard and nonmalleable but more fusible than steel.

Catenary arch: an arch having the same curved shape as that of a chain hanging freely from two fixed points-but turned upside down.

Centering: the temporary framework that supports a masonry arch while under construction.

Choir: the part of a church where services are sung.

Civil engineering: the designing and construction of public works such as dams, roads, canals, and bridges.

Cladding: a structure's outer skin that is attached to the frame after it is built.

Clerestory: a wall or story rising above an adjoining roof and containing windows.

Cofferdam: a watertight but open-to-the-air enclosure used primarily for excavating ground that is not deeply submerged.

Column: a vertical and usually round supporting pillar.

Compression: a force that shortens structural members by pressing or squeezing them together; opposite of tension.

Concrete: a hard building material made by mixing together a mineral aggregate (such as sand and gravel), a cementing material, and water.

Corbeling: successive masonry layers, each one projecting beyond the one immediately below it.

Cornice: a molded, horizontal projection that crowns the part to which it is attached.

Cramp: a device, usually of iron, that is used to pin timbers or stone blocks together.

Crenelation: a pattern of repeated dentations used, for example, in castle battlements.

Crossbeam: a beam that is set across another structural member.

Cross-bracing: a bracing system of intersecting diagonals.

Curtain wall: a non-load-bearing external wall that hangs from a skeleton frame.

Dead load: a constant load that results from a structure's weight, excluding occupants and contents.

Dome: usually a hemispherical ceiling or roof.

Dowel: a pin that fits into a hole in an abutting piece and prevents slippage.

Entablature: in classical architecture, a horizontal beam supported by columns.

Facing: a structure's outer masonry layer, used as ornamentation or for protection.

Flying buttress: a masonry structure that bears against an upright buttress on a church's external wall and directs downward the outward thrust of a vault.

Frame: the supporting structure, or skeleton, of a building.

Frieze: the part of an entablature between the cornice and the architrave.

Geodesic dome: a structure consisting of many light, straight elements, usually in tension, that form a grid shaped like a dome.

Girder: a large or principal beam in a structure.

Gnomon: an object positioned so that its shadow indicates the time of day.

Heading: the end of a horizontal, underground passageway or tunnel.

Heliostat: a mirrored instrument used to track the sun and reflect its light onto a receiver.

Hoop tension: the tension around the lower part of a dome.

Hypotenuse: the side opposite the right angle in a right-angled triangle.

Inclined plane: an inclined track on which heavy objects can be moved.

Joint: a place where two structural members are joined.

Keep: the stronghold of a castle.

Lintel: a short, horizontal beam that spans an opening.

Live load: the load beyond the weight of a structure itself; includes occupants and contents.

Load: the force placed on a structure by weight or wind pressure.

Load-bearing: capable of carrying a load in addition to its own weight.

Lock: a canal enclosure, with gates at both ends, used to lower or raise vessels from one level to another.

Macadamize: to construct a pavement by compacting layers of crushed stones on a convex roadbed and binding them together with cement or asphalt.

Machicolation: openings in a castle's parapet that are used for dropping missiles on enemies below.

Modular construction: construction that uses standardized dimensions or units.

Mortise: a cavity into which some other part, such as a tenon, is inserted.

Nave: the main part, or central aisle, of a church.

Oculus: something resembling an eye, especially a round opening at the crown of a dome.

Parabolic dish: a reflective structure that is dish- or bowl-shaped and focuses sunlight onto a receiver mounted above the center of the dish.

Parabolic trough: a reflective structure that has a curved, elongated shape and focuses sunlight onto a receiver running the length of the trough.

Pendentive: a triangular segment of vaulting that supports a circular dome over a square space.

Penstock: a conduit for water, especially one that controls the flow of water from a reservoir to a turbine.

Pentelic marble: marble that comes from Mount Pentelicus in Greece.

Photovoltaic cell: a device that is used to convert sunlight directly into electricity.

Pier: an upright structure, such as a column, a pillar, or a pilaster, that supports a vertical load.

Pilaster: a shallow, rectangular pier or column attached to a wall.

Portcullis: a retractable iron gate.

Precast: formed in the shape of a structural element, such as a concrete beam or panel, at a site other than where it will be used.

Prefabrication: factory production of standardized parts that can be assembled later at a construction site.

Prestressed concrete: concrete in which steel tendons have been introduced, stretched taut, and anchored at either

end. The ends pull together and thus create an upward force that counterbalances the downward force of the applied loads.

Purlin: a horizontal timber supporting the rafters in a roof.

Quadrant: one-quarter of a circle, or a device shaped like a quarter of a circle.

Reinforced concrete: concrete that has metal rods, wires, or bars embedded in it to add strength. Rivet: a metal bolt that is passed through holes in two metal plates and then hammered so that its plain end forms a second head and securely unites the plates.

Sarsen: a large sandstone block.

Semiconductor: a crystalline material, such as silicon, whose electrical conductivity is intermediate between an insulator and a metal.

Sill: a horizontal piece that is the lowest part of a framework or other supporting structure.

Slip form: a massive mold that is moved slowly up a structure, usually by hydraulic jacks, as concrete hardens within the mold.

Space frame: a three-dimensional structure composed of interconnected members in which stresses are equally distributed.

Span: the distance between supports in a structure.

Spillway: an opening or passage through which surplus water is released from a reservoir.

Stainless steel: a steel alloy that is highly resistant to rusting.

Steel: a commercial iron compound containing less carbon than cast iron and more than wrought iron, and which is highly malleable.

Stiffen: to increase a structure's resistance to deformation.

Stress: the force exerted as one body twists, pulls, presses, or pushes against another body; also, the intensity of this force as expressed in pounds per square inch.

Strut: a structural brace that resists pressure in the direction of its own length; can be vertical, horizontal, or diagonal.

Talus: a slope of soil and rock debris.

Tendon: in prestressed concrete, a steel band that is fitted into a concrete beam.

Tenon: a projection on a piece of wood or stone that is inserted into a mortise on another piece.

Tensile strength: the ability of a material to resist stretching forces.

Tension: a force that pulls outward on the members of a structure, stretching or lengthening them; the opposite of compression.

Thrust: the amount of force exerted by or on a structure.

Tongue-and-groove joint: a joint made when the tongue-like part on the edge of one object is fitted into a groove on the edge of another object.

Transept: the transverse arms of a cruciform church, usually separating the nave and the choir.

Truss: a framework of structural members, such as beams or girders, that strengthen each other and together form a long beam.

Vault: an arched structure, usually of masonry, that forms a roof or ceiling.

Viaduct: a bridge or series of bridges carrying a roadway or railway over an obstacle such as a valley.

Voussoir: a wedge-shaped block of stone used in a masonry arch or vault.

Waves: undulatory or rolling movements, including vibrations caused by an earthquake, that pass through air, water, and the earth.

Wind load: the force on a structure, or part of a structure, caused by the wind.

Wind shear: the stress on a structure when winds of different directions or velocities are close together.

Wind turbine: a machine that converts the force of the wind into electrical energy.

Wrought iron: a form of iron having a lower carbon content than steel or cast iron but which is tough and malleable.

Acknowledgments

The Book Division gratefully acknowledges the generous help of many individuals in preparing this volume, Our special thanks go to David P. Billington, Jr., Princeton University; Robert M. Vogel, retired curator of mechanical and civil engineering, Smithsonian Institution; William L. MacDonald; and David P. Billington and Robert Mark, Princeton University.

We would also like to thank Charles W. Boning, U.S. Geological Survey; Tim Brown, American Society of Civil Engineers; Pam Byer, CN Tower; John B, Carlson, Center for Archaeoastronomy; Scott Collins and Claude Wolff, Embassy of France; Craig Culp, American Wind Energy Association; Nathaniel Curtis, The Curtis Architectural Corporation; Darrell Dodge, Patrick Summers, and John Thornton, National Renewable Energy Laboratory; Neal Fitzsimons; Charles F. Gay and Barbara Isenburg, Siemens Solar Industries; Hermann Guenther of Daniel, Mann, Johnson & Mendenhall; James Harle, Alyeska Pipeline Service Company; John Hounslow, The Thames Barrier Operational Area; Folke T. Kihlstedt, Franklin and Marshall College; Mark Lehner, University of Chicago; Valerie Maftingley and Heather Yule, NGS London Office; Kerni E. Miller, KENETECH/U.S. Windpower; Kathleen Moenster, Jefferson National Expansion Historical Association; Michael Nylan, Bryn Mawr College; David O'Connor, University of Pennsylvania; Joseph Passoneau, Joseph Passoneau & Partners; Alison Porter, Eurotunnel; Julian Rhinehart, U.S. Bureau of Reclamation; Julian Richards, AC Archaeology; Jeffrey Stine, William Withuhn, and William Worthington, Jr., Smithsonian Institution; Homer A. Thompson, Princeton University; J. van Duivendijk, Royal Dutch Consulting Engineers; Richard M. Vogel, Tuffs University; Arthur Waldron, Naval War College.

At the National Geographic, we are indebted to the Pre-Press/Typographic Division, especially Jessica P. Norton, and to the Library and its News Collection, the Illustrations Library, and the Photographic Laboratory.

Credits

Index

MARVELS OF ENGINEERING

Published by the National Geographic Society

John M. Fahey, Jr., President and Chief Executive Officer
Gilbert M. Grosvenor, Chairman of the Board
Nina D. Hoffman, Executive Vice President;
    President, Book Publishing Group

Prepared by the Book Division

Kevin Mulroy, Senior Vice President and Publisher
Leah Bendavid-Val, Director of Photography
    Publishing and Illustrations
Marianne R. Koszorus, Director of Design
Barbara Brownell Grogan, Executive Editor
Elizabeth Newhouse, Director of Travel Publishing
Carl Mehler, Director of Maps

Staff for This Book

Barbara Levitt, Editor
Meredith C. Wilcox, Illustrations Editor
Cinda Rose, Art Director
Judith Klein, Contributing Editor
Mike Horenstein, Production Project Manager
Marshall Kiker, Illustrations Specialist
Cameron Zotter, Assistant Designer
Nicole DiPatrizio, Al Morrow, Design Assistants
Jennifer A. Thornton, Managing Editor
Gary Colbert, Production Director

Special Contributors: Jennifer Conrad Seidel (text),
Connie D. Binder (index)

Manufacturing and Quality Management

Christopher A. Liedel, Chief Financial Officer
Phillip L. Schlosser, Vice President
John T. Dunn, Technical Director
Chris Brown, Director
Maryclare Tracy, Manager
Nicole Elliott, Manager

Founded in 1888, the National Geographic Society is
one of the largest nonprofit scientific and educational
organizations in the world. It reaches more than 285
million people worldwide each month through its
official journal, NATIONAL GEOGRAPHIC, and its four
other magazines; the National Geographic Channel;
television documentaries; radio programs; films;
books; videos and DVDs; maps; and interactive
media. National Geographic has funded more than
8,000 scientific research projects and supports an
education program combating geographic illiteracy.

For more information, please call
1-800-NGS LINE (647-5463)
or write to the following address:

National Geographic Society
1145 17th Street N.W.
Washington, D.C. 20036-4688 U.S.A.

Visit us online at www.nationalgeographic.com

For information about special discounts
for bulk purchases, please contact
National Geographic Books Special Sales:
ngspecsales@ngs.org

For rights or permissions inquiries,
please contact National Geographic Books Subsidiary
Rights: ngbookrights@ngs.org

Library of Congress Cataloging-in-Publication Data
Marvels of engineering.
  p. cm.
Includes index.
  ISBN 978-1-4262-0133-2 − ISBN 978-1-4262-0134-9
1. Engineering—History. I. National Geographic Society (U.S.)
  TA15.M37 2007
  620−dc22

                                          2007042934

ISBN: 978-1-4262-0133-2
ISBN: 978-1-4262-0134-9 (dlx)
Printed in U.S.A.